THE FEELING FOR NATURE IN ENGLISH PASTORAL POETRY. A THESIS

Published @ 2017 Trieste Publishing Pty Ltd

ISBN 9780649582167

The Feeling for Nature in English Pastoral Poetry. A Thesis by J. Ingram Bryan

Edited by Trieste Publishing Pty Ltd.
Cover @ 2017

www.triestepublishing.com

J. INGRAM BRYAN

THE FEELING FOR NATURE IN ENGLISH PASTORAL POETRY. A THESIS

The Feeling for Nature in English Pastoral Poetry

BY

J. INGRAM BRYAN
M.A., M. LITT., PH.D.

A THESIS

Presented to the Faculty of the Graduate School of the
University of Pennsylvania in Partial Fulfilment
of the Requirements for the Degree of
Doctor of Philosophy, 1907.

TOKYO
KYO-BUN-KWAN
1908

CONTENTS

CHAPTER I

THE NATURE OF PASTORAL POETRY

THERE are doubtless many lovers of literature to whom the attempt to discover a feeling for nature in Pastoral Poetry, will seem a hopeless endeavor. In the history of imaginative and emotive verse, the pastoral somehow appears to have been looked upon as a mode of writing quite incapable of any genuine sympathy with the real things of life, least of all with nature herself, the subject of the pastoral being seldom alluded to, save as a synonym for cold and affected conventionality. Yet some of the greatest poets essayed this mode, and in the shepherd's garb, failed not to make " the too much loved earth more lovely." *

Whether the poet be able so to project himself into nature, as to cause her to interpret herself to him, must assuredly depend more upon the genius of the artist himself, than upon the mode of his expression. The pastoral poet, not less than any poet, must in some way discover that quality interwoven with the essential texture of creation, which we call beauty, for only as he does so, is he true to nature and to poetry. We venture, therefore, upon the 'a priori' statement that all verse not founded on nature lacks the quality of poetry, and becomes only a convenient way of talking nonsense.

It is undoubtedly true that in the days of its greatest popularity, under the auspices of syncophants and courtiers, the pastoral often became either diluted into the ridiculously fanciful, if not the

---

* " Apology for Poetry " by Sir Phillip Sidney.

absurdly impossible, but this defection in deference
to the glamor of courts, was a negation of its birthright, and never the prevailing note of the great
pastoralists whose magnificent outbursts of rural
song, charged with all the tender beauties of nature
and alive with the delicate emotions of rustic love,
pipe melodiously down the orchestras of time.   An
instrument that has discoursed such eloquent music,
and to whose sweet piping even princes among the
poets have attuned their ears, must surely have
possessed some virtue capable of stealing an echo
from nature's heart.

It is important to inquire at the outset, what is
meant by the term "pastoral" as applied to poetry,
and to grasp as far as possible the essential features
that distinguish it from other types of literature.
Satisfactory definitions are always difficult to frame,
and in matters of art, often impossible.   Pastoral
poetry in particular, is one of those elusive phenomena that cannot be defined in terms which would
satisfy a logician.   It were as easy to describe a
mass of cloud and shower moving down a mountainous coastline and over an arm of the sea, lit up
where the sun breaks through, by a wonderful and
delicate inweaving of the subtlest harmonies of color.
Equally subtle are the effects upon which the pastoral
depends; and we must not insist upon a faultless
definition of it, any more than upon a faultless
example of the pastoral itself.   Poetry so capable of
being charged with nature's sweetness, cannot be
caught, penned up and numbered like a flock of
sheep; it has a habit of breaking bounds and may
be found in any guise of poetry or even prose.[*]

---

[*] "Elizabethan Lyrics," by F. E. Schelling, Litt. D., P. 52.

If the word "pastoral" be a generic term denoting a literary mode and not a special literary form, its comprehensive possibilities for an appreciation of nature are at once evident, and to inquire how far the poets have succeeded in using their opportunity, is our present task. It is upon the results of this inquiry that our definition of the pastoral must be based, rather than upon any preconceived theory as to what they ought to have done.

Among the Greeks where the star of pastoral song first arose, the term idyl which was the earliest literary form to exhibit the pastoral motive, sufficiently explains what they conceived to be its nature. The idyl of the Alexandrians is a little picture of rustic or town life, made up of legends of the gods, or passages from personal experience, the poem flowing in a somewhat reflective strain. In the idyls of the Greeks we hear nature speaking with a human voice conveying impressions of rustic emotion and environment, and in a delicate, simple, but none the less poetic manner.

In the Latin eclogue which was an attempt at imitating the Greek idyl, we note the germs of Grecian idealization beginning to develope but no evidence of ability to maintain the Greek appreciation of nature. Virgil, the first among the Romans to try this kind of poetry, departed from the original intent of the idyl, and was not entirely successful in reproducing the sweet simplicity and delicate sentiment of Theocritus. In the days of later Italy when artistically the pastoral reached a high degree of literary culture in the hands of Bocaccio, Guarini and Tasso, it still remained as artificial in its conception as in the days when Virgil used it to cover the experiences of his fictitious beings, or to paint the cold conceits of an imperious age. Though popular in Italy, the pastoral was really an exotic on Italian soil and never regained the vigorous freshness of the youth it enjoyed among the sunny hills of Sicily. The poets of France, Germany and Spain, caught the pastoral craze of the Italians, and through most of the renaissance and later periods, these countries abounded in pastoral literature of all kinds, but none of the writers ever attained to a conception of its native simplicity. It was through the influence of the French and Italian pastoralists, more especially Sanazzaro, Tasso, and Marot, that bucolic verse was introduced into England where it became a cult reaching its climax between the years 1580 to 1590. Notwithstanding the tendency of the pastoral in the chequered course of its history, to become purely an artificial product, yet in England, in the hands of its earlier essayists at least, it was on the whole human and real, indicating as keen a sympathy with nature as any other contemporary poetry.

The pastoral could not, however, resist the false literary taste of later times, and the breaking away from nature is echoed in such conventional definitions as that of Drayton who says that "Pastorals are a species of poetry, signifying feigned dialogues or other speeches in verse, fathered on husbandmen or shepherds." Pope whose youthful flirtations with the pastoral muse became notorious, likewise limits her poetic expression to conventional verse: "A pastoral is the imitation of the actions of a shepherd or one considered under that character. . . The table is simple and the manner not too polite nor too rustic."*

In No. 22 of the Guardian, a paper much given of dissertation upon this mode of writing, there is a

---

* Essay prefixed to Pope's Pastorals.

description of the pastoral, which is interesting as
evidence of what the popular conception was at
a time when its possibilities on English soil had
been fairly tested : " Pastoral poetry not only.
amuses the fancy the most delightfully, but it is
likewise more indebted to it than to any other sort
whatever. It transports us into a kind of fairy-land
where one's ears are soothed with the melody of
birds, bleating flocks and purling streàms ; our eyes
are enchanted with flowery meadows and springing
greens ; we are laid under cool shades and entertained
with all the sweet freshness of nature, It is a dream ;
it is a vision which we wish may be real and we
believe that it is true." Here again we breathe the
chilling atmosphere of that pseudo-classic unreality
upon which the bucolic Muse had been forced to
live during her rambles through Italy and France,
and from the effects of which she never recovered
beneath the more sombre skies of Britain. The
matter and manner of rustic life was affected by the
poet, not for the sake of accurate description or
appreciation of nature, but purely as an artistic
device for portraying the interests and emotions of
the poet himself, or of the sophisticated society in
which he lived. Against this counterfeit tendency
which makes the pastoral no more than a play of
city folk at country life, comes the accustomed
modern protest of Mr. Ruskin who maintains that
" all good poetry descriptive of rural life is essentially
pastoral "—a definition manifestly based upon what
he assumes pastoral poetry ought to be rather than
upon what its history shows it to be.

From what has been said it will be readily seen
how very early the pastoral began to wander from
its original idea. Though the Greek idyl contained
the germs of its later idealization among the Romans

and Italians, the writings of Theocritus reveal a sincere expression of man's delight in rural simplicity and contentment, idealized sufficiently to admit them into the realm of art. Their leading motive is a genuine delight in the beauty of nature, mixed with a feeling of sympathy and respect for whatever is noble, honest and wholesome, in lowly life. As the spirit of art became more general, commonplace poets began to court the pastoral Muse,—an ambition in which even the most consumate literary artist can barely succeed, and naturally the subject under such treatment, often drifted beyond the limits of art, into an idealization of the insincere, the unreal, the solely artificial, the purely fanciful and imaginary. The pastoral assumed various shades of meaning according to the changing tendencies of the life and literature of each particular age. The majority of those who have taken the pipe as the instrument of their music, have not confined themselves to the simple songs of the hills or the hamlet. As it was with Virgil, so it has been with most of his successors in Italy and imitators in England; we note how soon the pastoral in their hands is no longer content with ideal descriptions of nature nor the buoyant delights of rural life, but is taken up, not only with fancies gleaned from classical mythology in which the people of the time had no faith, but also indulges in satirical and other irrelevant allusions to politics, history, religious influences and controversies, or whatever was uppermost in the mind of the time. Indeed the popularity of the pastoral was often largely due to its being one of the most convenient pretexts for the expression of what would otherwise be embarrassing, and therefore became an easy refuge for the satirist or the flatterer.

This want of mastery over the subject evinced by so many poets, has led some critics to aver that the pastoral is a mode of writing peculiar to the more remote and naïve periods of history before the growth of great centers of civilization, when the chief wealth and influence of the country depended on flocks and fields. Historically, however, such poetry has appeared only at times of the most advanced human refinement, as, for example, in Greece where it was not produced for centuries after Homer, and then only at a period when the people had arisen to a more artistic and poetic appreciation of nature apart from her utilitarian aspects. And what is true of Greece, is true of every country where the pastoral has been cultivated. Hence the naïveté and frolicsomeness that make up so much of the charm and spirit of pastoral poetry, are not the relics of any one age or state of society, but the permanent characteristics of human nature itself; man may be content to find his amusements in cities, but for his play he prefers the country with its open vistas and relaxing moods.

Looking back, therefore, over the whole course of its history, and judging it by the treatment of its most ardent admirers and friends, the pastoral may be defined as an idealized portrayal of rural life. Such a theme naturally lends itself to poetic treatment. And the distinguishing trait of the feeling for nature in pastoral poetry as contrasted with the same feeling in poetry of other kinds, consists largely in this love of fantastic idealization and rapturous contemplation of the more apparent and homely phases of rural life and scenery. On a background of nature we have brilliant impressionistic touches of human life as the poet divines it: the entrancement of man's loves and joys, not always uncolored by the passion of his sins and sorrows, but with an undertone of optimism pervading all. The pastoral view of nature represents the happy, if highly idealized, medium between the intellectual abstractions of Shelley on the one hand, and the erotic sensuousness of Byron on the other, and so belongs to a manner different from either. To the pastoralist nature is fused with a human emotion that lends her sweet mysteries; she is essentially good at heart, and the more unartificial and unconventional the better. While individualism plays a prominent part on the face of nature, it is never coldly subjective or exclusive; for the predominant note is social and spiritual.

These traditional traits Theocritus fixed upon the pastoral for all time. With him it was a song out of the heart of nature, but a nature thrilled with human sympathies. The singing matches are for rustic wagers, a soft white lamb or a carven drinking bowl made from beech or maple. The bout of rude banterings between rival swains, the sad lament of a lover for unrequited or deceived affection, the dirge of his fellows around the tomb of some dead shepherd, the ecstatic absorption in some amorous theme,—these dominant phases of the pastoral combine to show that it arose out of intuitions with regard to nature, and represented a folksong distinct inherently from other kinds of poetry.

Love is the natural atmosphere of pastoral nature; and its joys are not indifferent to the shadows that always follow light. But its faint tincture of Bohemianism does not exclude a love of domesticity emphasizing the exhaltation of that contentment which comes with a sufficiency for the wants of the outward and the inward man; nor yet virtue of facing calmly, and braving honestly, life's uncertain-

ties ; the duty of delighting in, and taking refreshment from, natural beauty. And, withal, there is
nothing of the profundity that characterizes other
modes of poetry : simply the love and joy and
beauty, that play constantly over the rippling
surfaces of life. If this mode of literature reveals no
haunting sense of immanent Deity, and rejoices in,
rather than fears, the gods, it nevertheless expresses
the voice and the vision of Him who doubtless
created man to love and exult in the hale old earth,—
its birds and beasts and flowers ; and not least, its
May-time,

> " The spring-time, the only happy ring-time."

And thus in pastoral poetry there is a blending,
under charmingly idealized, treatment of many of the
more dominant notes of other kinds of poetry. Nature
in the epic is a prevailingly descriptive element ; in
the lyric proper she is persistently the voice of
subjective, individual passion ; in the drama she is
often but a background or a symbol subordinated
to a reflection or interpretation of human action : in
the pastoral she is more often a happy combination
of all these elements,—an idyl, a song, a passion,
bursting from the heart of nature, with a message
of joy or triumph from some happy human thing to
others of its kind in the same old world.

And if it be objected that too many of those who
have cultivated this mode of literature, allowing
idealization to run riot with art, have made country
life unreal and the present ridiculous, we can only
say that the defect is in the poet rather than in his
theme. Those poets that from their fairy garden
nooks have vainly attempted to imitate nature, the
while mentally wandering through the fairy
labyrinths of some impossible arcadia, are far

outshone by the few great ones, eminently artistic
and sane : Theocritus, Tasso, Spenser, Browne,
and others in that long and illustrious line of nature's
prophets who have lifted the poetry of rural life
above the conceits of a false classicism, and the
silver tinklings of a courtly lyre.

It is, therefore, apparent that love of nature,
especially nature in relation to man, was one of the
main emotions to which the most significant of the
pastoralists endeavored to appeal. And though it
was often an extremely limited phase of nature,—a
nature cultivated and subdued by man,—evincing a
horror of all wild and mountainous wastes and
based upon imagination rather than upon observation, yet it revealed the aspects of nature that
appealed most to the people of the time ; and even
art cannot ignore the people.

Thus by a love of nature always made sweet by
human love as the central theme ; decorated with
wit and satire ; painted with allegory and skillful
use of mythology, pastoral literature created and
maintained a popularity that continued until a truer
poetry of nature arose to meet the deeper longings
of men.

Living, as we do, in the cold light of modern
criticism, surrounded by different standards of taste
and feeling, we are scarcely capable of doing justice
to a time which loved to revel in regions of simple
fancy ; and whose cultivation and appreciation of the
pastoral were genuine and not affected, widespread
and not local.

It is indeed true that, generally speaking, the
bucolic Muse has not met with many responsive
souls in the hard, work-a-day world of modern
Europe and America. For the indifferent mass,
with their second-hand impressions, it has been

enough that the pastoral is an exotic, without any regard to the main truth as to whether it is good poetry. But to those not given up the baldest and most sordid realism, pastoral poetry has a voice that murmurs music, soft and enthralling as that of a slow-flowing river through the reeds. And if the pastoral has attained unto a very high place in literary art, and has succeeded in raising the charm of country life to a height reached only by a poetic imagination ; if its poetry lends a stimulus to the heart and a solace to the brain, and becomes to some extent a realization of nature's color and music, imparting to man a measure of her beauteous and consoling harmonies, then assuredly it fills a place that cannot be left empty without marring many a graceful and picturesque outline in that temple which wisdom, time, and beauty, build to poetry.*

---

* See E. Gosse ; Essay on Pastoral Poetry.

CHAPTER II

THE FEELING FOR NATURE IN THE GREEK
SOURCES OF THE ENGLISH PASTORAL

FROM the time that men began to congregate in cities, and to became absorbed in the wearying artificiality of material pursuits, they have cherished a longing to infuse the dull monotony of existence with the inspiration of sights and sounds from country life. As the activities of civilization increase in the busy centers of competition, the tired soul of man looks back enviously to the days of his rustic forefathers whose quiet existence in the shady groves and upland pastures, he imagines to have been a state of innocence and ease. Those inherited memories of man's age-long existence in woods and fields, come back to him in the midst of his strenuous endeavor,—sweet as the recollections of childhood. Poetry, painting, all true art, is but the cry of man after the beauty inherent in nature independently of himself, and without an appreciation of which, there is famine in his soul. It was thirst for the refreshment which nature alone can offer, that gave rise to pastoral poetry; it was the revolt of the heart against mechanical views of life; the protest of love against expediency; of art against selfishness.

A poet, therefore, could find no theme more agreeable to his genius than the contemplation and interpretation of those aspects of nature most relaxing to the jaded minds and bodies of a satiated society. If all the poets that have undertaken it, had but gone directly to nature, instead of copying from one another, the historians of the pastoral would have been saved the dreary waste of artificiality and unreasoning idealism, that characterizes so much of its career.

This tendency of the pastoral toward extreme idealism, has, however, an optimistic message, for it simply means that life and literature are one, and human. It has ever been a feature of progressive humanity that it looks backward or forward to some distant ideal age for alleviation of difficulty, and for inspiration of life. Dissatisfaction with the present is the most significant note that any department of life can utter. Now it was this groping after better things, that very early gave the pastoral its Arcadian drift. And the ennui of the society of courts and people of leisure, lent all the potency of its cultivated circles to encourage this idealization of rural life ; they longed for the country but they could not tolerate the peasant, so they endeavored to enjoy in imagination what they could not possess in reality. If they did not make the country, they at least peopled it with beings acceptable to the fancy of the age.

Of the aspect of the pastoral as a pervading principle of social evolution, history furnished abundant examples. Virgil fancied that Augustus was bringing back the age of gold—the early Christians lived with all their feelings intensified by yearly or even daily anticipation of the second coming of Christ. The Crusaders filled all Christendom with the belief that if the East could be delivered from the rule of the infidel, the millennium would immediately set in. The Puritans looked forward to a reign of saints upon the earth, when some epoch-making catastrophe should plunge into the lake of brimstone all whose talents and manners gave grace and cheerfulness to existence. The French revolutionists indulged in a similar dream, though in place of the saints, they set up the goddess of reason, persuaded themselves that in the formula of Liberty, Fraternity, and Equality, the means were revealed to them of inaugurating an immediate and satisfactory condition of society. Italy imagined when once it was united and independent, it would be a new garden of Eden,

> " White with the dew and the rime,
> When the morning of God comes down."

The same wondrous tale has been taken up by Socialistic visionaries who imagine that a new economic regime can be established, under which everybody can be as rich as he wishes, and nobody shall be any richer than his neighbor.   Comte dreamed that the days of the Christian Church were numbered, and that all Paris would presently be a sort of Salvation Army skipping and singing hymns to the glory of universal humanity.

Now if literature be an interpretation of life, it must needs reflect, if not fully portray, these movements of time ; and pastoral poetry not less than any other mode of literature, has done so, and with a saner effect, and a more general relief to society, than any of the more directly romantic compositions of the period in which it flourished.

It was quite natural, therefore, that, in the days of Grecian disintegration when religion was base and patriotism dead, and the Arbiter of national destiny had removed the Capital from Athens to Alexandria ;—when the age of prose had been struck with academic langour, and the fires upon the altar of the Attic Muse were smouldering, the genius of pastoral music should arise to rekindle that flame under whose spring warmth Greek life should revive, and Greek poetry put forth its last, but not least lovely, blossom.

Under the inspiration of Theocritus, the people of Greece, with pathetic intensity, turned from idle and luxurious pleasures, to contemplating the innocent delights of rural life, seeking an ideal refinement in rustic nature, and lavishing all the splendor of their genius upon the idealization of ploughmen, shepherds, and fishermen, who afterwards became the serf population of the Roman empire.

It was in the little island of Cos whose hills are bathed by the blue haze and whose shores are washed by the Greek seas, that pastoral poetry was born. Mysterious indeed must have been the circumstances which attended that event in the history of literature. Mr. Edmund Gosse, in his admirable essay upon this subject, with characteristic grace thus describes the joy of its birth: " We still hear the echoes of that pleasant music which the poets made that day in Greece long ago when Eucritus and Theocritus, walking under the shadow of the Coan elms and seeing the light gleam on the trembling poplars, were met in the bush of the noon-tide heat by the Cydonian ' best of men.' The larks were silent in the stubble, the lizard was basking motionless in the glaring wall, while Lycidas sang of the goat-herd in the miraculous cedarn chest, and the poet answered in tender appeal to Pan to heal the heart-wound of a learned and unhappy friend. The goddess who stood by smiling when these songs were over, with her brown hand full of corn and poppies, was no other than the buxom muse of pastoral poetry." Thus was brought forth the youngest child of Greek genius,

destined to outlive the permanency of the hills and
streams along which she loved to loiter.

Though we may find among the Greek poets, the
elements that go to make the pastoral, and even in
' polumelos'—(Πολύμηλος) the Homeric prenomen
for a sheep-grazing country,—see a picture of the
woolly bleaters that whiten all the plain, yet it was
through Theocritus that the idyl first reached that
point in its evolution, where could be seen its
literary possibilities for the expression of pastoral
life.

Born amidst those beauteous natural scenes that
everywhere grace the Sicillian landscape, and which
through all the changes of time, have never lost
their sunny charm, Theocritus loved to contemplate
and to idealize the lives of his native herdsmen, in
whose songs on the lone bay of Syracuse, we may
still hear echo of the pipes of Pan. Through every
line of his delightful picturing, the perennial sunlight
floods with its joyous glow, and as the poet wanders
among these sunlit hills and valleys of his delight-
some island, over its free and open farms, he catches
music from the voices of young men and maidens,
and blending it with that of snow-fed streams from
the heart of mighty Etna, he makes a song that
charms every lover of poetry. The rustic melodies
of the Dorian peasants whose faith in the magic of
pools where the Naiads dance, was still alive, and
Theocritus sang with a poetic utterance so full and
true that every scene of idyllic life framed between
Etna and the distant sea, in his mind became one
golden world of pastoral. It is a world made happy,
not only by human scenes and voices, but by an
ardent and delicate contemplation of animal life in
its more joyous moods: "Sweet are the voices of
the calves; and sweet the heifer's lowing; sweet

plays the shepherd on the shepherd's pipe, and sweet is the echo."* He observes "the little foxes stealing through the grape vines," and that " where rank grasses grow, the bees are humming everywhere," and how, in the still heat of the Sicilian afternoon, " On shady boughs the burnt Cicadas piped their shrill and ceaseless note ".†

Theocritus also divined and interpreted the life of woods and mountains with a fine and characteristic simplicity. The opening lines of the first idyl are fragrant with the resinous atmosphere of pines towering above the spires of the slender cypress trees and showing black against the gray olive groves :—" Sweet is the music of rustling pines above the springs, and sweet the piping of Shepherds ".‡

Mythology was the Greek method of interpreting nature, and in the mind of Theocritus, her sights and sounds melt into human forms and break into human speech. The inconstant sea with the charm of its summer waves, more fickle and light than thistle down, becomes Galatea bearing a message to those pained with the vicissitudes of love ; and in the music of falling water and the murmur of eddying streams, is the nymph's amoretti. In this way everything in nature is idealized into human shape and speech, whether of the mountains or the sea, " each a mighty voice "; and everywhere man's sense of beauty is touched with a subtle power, and his spirit soothed by the majesty of classical repose.

There is in Theocritus that breath of perpetual spring which one still feels along the shores of the Mediterranean, as for instance, at Amalphi or

---

* Idyl I.; † Idyl X.
‡ " ἁδύ τι τό Ψιθύρισμα καὶ ἁ Πίτυς, αἰπολε Τήνα,"

Sorrento. The stars of his turquoise sky are not so numberless or so brilliant as among the poets of the frosty northlands, but they trill out a message over the stillness of the sea and the whispering of the night-winds, that indicates a due appreciation of the heavenly expanse :

> " Now rests the deep, now rest the wandering winds,
> But in my heart the anguish will not rest,
> While for her love I pine, who stole my sweetness,
> And made me less than virgin among maids."*
>
> J. A. SYMONDS.

While the interest of Theocritus in nature is largely associated with his relation to man, he is at the same time imbued with a deep sympathy for nature in herself, and often hymns the music of common things as in themselves beautiful. True, his attitude toward nature, in this respect, is for the most part but faintly revealed, yet even a slight indication of the ' Nature-feeling ' is as much a proof of its presence, as if it were spread on with a lavish hand. Though but ten of his thirty-two idyls are strictly pastoral, the feeling for nature is as constant as the human interest and the literary charm.

In the second idyl of Theocritus we have a lyric of bliss, wherein is distilled the sweetness of all pastoral literature. It may be true that even here, he does not widely diverge from the Greek habit of interpreting nature through man, and is more concerned with nature as the expression of law in beauty and form, in order and life, than as the echo of a universal voice and the revelation of a universal life ; but it may be safely said that he does go further than most

---

* ἠνίδεσιγὰ μὲνπόντος, σιγῶτι δ'ἀῆται·
ἁ δ' ἐμὰ οὐ σιγὰ στέρνων ἔνοσθεν ἀνία,
ἀλλ' ἐπὶ τήνῳ πᾶσα καταίθομαι, ὃς με τάλαιναν
ἀντί γυναικὸς ἔθηκε κακὰν καὶ ἀπάρθενον ἦμεν.

of the Greek poets, in showing a genuine love of nature for her own sake, rather than as an illustration of his art. To Theocritus, nature is ever whispering of her mysteries, which is the first indication of a consciousness of the infinitude of knowledge and the endlessness of Good. Nature in this poet, suggests dreams that wander forth beyond the orbits of the stars ; and under his inspiring touch words of melody rise naturally as flowers from a field.

One is loath to turn from this restful scene where the scent of honey is on the winds and all about is the shining quiet of the summer noon, to the less alluring haunts of succeeding pastoralists. If subsequent devotees of the bucolic muse must needs copy and elaborate, we may well ask why they did not at least go to the fountain-head and drink deeply at the source of pastoral song ? The answer is obvious. There is a sunniness, a lightsomeness, and an artistic appreciation of nature in those Greek pastorals, that it would be vain to hope for in the more umbrageous landscape of the North where the eye travels through vistas of leafy boughs to still, secluded crofts, and dwells on pastures where slow-moving oxen feed. The English pastoral with its tame, cultivated gardens, foggy skies, and boisterous shores, has little of the everlasting laughter of the Sicilian sea and sky. It lacks, too, that matchless robe of silver mist which the olive orchards give ; it has never felt the breath of perennial spring.

Moreover, in looking to the Greeks for inspiration, the English pastoral writers labored under the disadvantage of a different point of view. They seem altogether unaware that theirs is a different world— a world grown older by at least 2000 years. They did not realize that not only was the Greek mode of expression different from their own, but even the same words had another meaning. The conciseness, simplicity, and almost prosaic accuracy of classical descriptive art, ill-became poets of a more florid age, and the mythological characters which represented real thoughts to the hearers and readers of Theocritus, lost their vigor and charm in the ears of those who had no appreciation of the profound emotions implied in such conceptions as Pan and Galatea. Thus the music chrystallized into Greek song vanished in the process of translation into another tongue and age.

Even the Greek followers of Theocritus failed to catch the melody of his honeyed numbers, and their writings are too cold, affected and insipid to be important in our present consideration, especially as they had little or no influence upon the English pastoral feeling for nature. The best known names are those of Bion and Moschus, both of whom remind one more of the grammarian than the poet, and smack more of the study than of the fields ; and the much later Greek pastoral of " Daphnis and Chloe " by Longus, has practically no bearing upon our subject.

CHAPTER III

THE LATIN AND ITALIAN SOURCES OF THE ENGLISH PASTORAL

THE feeling for nature in the Latin and Italian pastoralists has an important bearing upon the subject before us, because it was through them that this mode of writing found its way into England. Neither among the Romans nor Italians did the pastoral ever feel wholly at home ; therefore it never dealt seriously with the life of the people. The cultivated Roman had little sympathy with the lower orders of his time, and the Latin poets soon found that the pure gold of innocent rustic song had to be mixed with such alloy as would give it currency in Rome.

Later on, in the days of the Renaissance when the Italian gentry had a greater love for country life, and spent a large part of their time at their rural villas, the pastoral drama became popular in Italy, and the rich, when called to town for business or pleasure, listened with delight to the idealized reflections of rural life, which they heard upon the stage ; but the pastoral, in so far as it was a true reflection of nature, never met with a wide reception in Italy.

The Roman of Virgillian days was not greatly different from the Italian of the days of Tasso. Though the Italian may have re-birth, he never seems to experience new birth ; and so the renaissance was to him what its name implies,—a ' re-bringing-forth ' of what was before. Even Greek influence, therefore, could not alter the Italian temperament, nor Theocritus give to Virgil the warm-blooded freedom and beauty of the Sicilian fields.

The Eclogues of Virgil, which were published in 37 B. C., afford us the first example of Latin pastoral writing. They are brief and polished but lack the natural idealization and exquisite art of the later Italians. Virgil is a close imitator of Theocritus, but he leaves out the Greek naturalness of feeling and freshness of manner. Even the names of his shepherds are Greek, and the landscape of Sicily is mixed with life and scenery from the marshy flat lands of Lombardy. The delectable sweetness ($\dot{\alpha}\delta\upsilon$) which the great Syracusan sees in nature, vanishes with Virgil into veiled allusions to Roman politics and the servile adulation of courts,—an infection that tainted the pastoral through much of its subsequent history. The introduction of personal allegorical figures by Virgil, offered so great an attraction to satirists, and so excellent a means of eulogy to seekers after patronage, that in time the genuine swains and herdmaidens, were overshadowed by a world of inane artificiality.

Virgil, unlike the Greeks, had just enough antiquity behind him to come betwixt him and the face of nature. He did not see it at first hand, with his own eyes, but through those who had written before him, until the very air of his pastorals, is colored with the hues of Greece. Yet, with the exception of Lucretius, Virgil has more real appreciation of nature in herself, than any of the Roman poets before or after him, and was so recognized by his friend and contemporary, Horace who wrote of him :

> " Molle atque facetum
> Virgilio amnerunt gaudentes rure Camoenae."

Notwithstanding the imitative and generally conventional character of his eclogues, there are times when he breaks away after something that he has seen for himself, as when he describes his farm as covered with bare stones, and tells how the " slimy bulrushes and the river Mincio, weave for his green banks a fringe ef tender reeds......"

In the fifth eclogue of Virgil, Menalcas says to Mopsus who has been playing to him :

> " Such is thy song to me, O Singer divine,
> As is sleep upon the grass to weary men."—

to which Mopsus replies :

> " What gifts shall I render thee for such a song ? "
> For not so delightful to me is the sighing of the coming
>   south wind,
> Nor the beating of the billows upon the shore,
> Nor the sound of streams down-falling through rocky
>   glens."

In the Georgics of Virgil there is also a large background of landscape wherein the plains of Mantua and the Campania lie spread out before us, while the intense skies of Italy burn overhead.

But the peasant who was a god to Homer and Theocritus, and a priest to Virgil, among the aristocracy of later times fell from his high estate, and a new pastoral poetry arose to his rescue. This new poetry labored under the disadvantage of being in its origin simply an academic hobby, for the Italians began to write pastorals only because Virgil wrote eclogues. Virgil was made the object of a cult ; it was proper to do what Virgil did.

Those, however, who attempted to imitate Virgil, had not been born and raised amid those rural scenes which had so penetrated the poet's mind that he could not help setting them down in the middle of Sicily. The new pastoralists were content to write pretty verses sprinkled with classical names, and with little or no appreciation of the beauties of nature. The pastoral now became the mouthpiece of lovers

and haters, friendships and jealousies ; it was at one
time a courtly panegyric, and at another a political
or ecclesiastical satire. Yet out of these confused
attempts, something more genuine arose, until the
pastoral, like other forms of poetry, became at last
an embodied sigh of relief at having got out of the
fighting and lasting Middle Ages, into the purer air
of modern sympathy with nature and human life.

Throughout the twelfth and thirteenth centuries a
new and apparently independent stream of poetry
mingled with the current of classical pastoral tradition. The communal and chivalric poetry, both
lyrical and narrative, of the Middle Ages, took partly
the form of the pastoral lyric, called by the French,
' Pastourelle', which represented the courting of
a shepherdess by a knight or man of rank, and cor-
responded to the Italian ' Pastoralia ' in which the
rustic was wooed by a scholar. These forms became
universally popular, and are to be found in all the
romance literatures of the mediaeval and renaissance
periods.

It is in Italy that we notice the first fusion of these
newer models with the older classical forms, expand-
ing at last into the romance and the pastoral drama.
Perhaps the earliest example of an imitation of the
ancient classical idyl by the Italians, is that of the
eclogue purporting to have passed between Dante
and Virgilius a teacher of grammar at Bologna,—a
species also well illustrated in the songs of Sachetti's
peasant girls, and in the pastoral poems of Amalphei.
It is in Dante, however, that we have the first sincere
reversion to the language of the people, which shows
genuine sympathy with pastoral life : " What time
the hoar-frost on the ground simulates its white
sister, but quickly wears away, the little peasant,
who all things lacks, leaves his bed and looks out at

the whitened country ; whence he slaps his thigh, and going back into the house, tramps up and down like a mob that knows not what it does.   Then he renews his spirits ; hope revives as he beholds how in a few hours the world has changed its face.   And now he takes his crook and forth he drives his sheep from pools to pasture ".*   Who that has visited the winter haunts of Dante at Casertino, does not recognize the truth of this picture, or if in summer, that of the Shepherd under the trees while the " Swarms of daytime insects yield to the evening quiet ".   This note which was struck by Dante in making the peasant a mirror and complement of his environment, is the secret after which pastoral poetry had been long unconsciously feeling, and faint echoes of its music can be heard in subsequent pastoral verse.

With the Renaissance came in the Humanistic revival of classical studies beginning with Petrarch (1304–1374) whose twelve poems, entitled " Carmen Bucolicum " are the first of a long series of imitations of the pastoral manner of Virgil, some of which are remarkably beautiful.   Petrarch follows his master as closely in spirit as in form, even to the adoption of the eulogistic device, and with a dignity and moral elevation that had no idea of transcribing in Latin verse the actual peasant life of Italy. Mantuan, the fellow-townsman of Petrarch, continued the process of fossilizing the bucolic dialogue in classical verse, using it largely as a medium for moral and satirical effect.   This Carmelite monk, however, knew intimately the Italian rustic, and prefering the charms of country life to the splendor of a corrupt society in the days of Leo X, did, notwithstanding his ultra classicism and Roman

---

* Dante, Inferno, Canto XXIV.

spirit, originate a new pastoral in Italy, which was much admired by Shakespeare and copied by Spenser.

In Bocaccio, the Humanistic friend of Petrarch, we have an amplification of pastoral tendency, that produced the newer forms to which reference has already been made ; and which carried the pastoral further away from sympathy with nature. Most of the pastoral writings of Bocaccio are associated with his life at Naples, and directly or indirectly with his love for the princess Maria, all of which is veiled in his prose pastoral allegory, " Fiammetta ".

One of these newer forms which tended to check the growth of a feeling for nature in pastoral poetry, now came into prominence in the shape of Pastoral Drama. The " Drammi Pastorali " of Italian idyllic poetry, originated in the fifteenth century, when the public recitation of Italian eclogues was for the first time divorced from religious ceremonies, with which up to that time it had been connected. The result was a new type of drama, neither tragic nor in the nature of comedy, but a combination that assumed the name of " pastoral ". Its setting was in the blissful age of gold and gods, and the " dramatis personae " were restricted to shepherds, nymphs, and other characters of pastoral precedent.

The earliest attempt to represent a fable of this kind in a dramatic way, was, in the " Cafolo " of Corregio, and later came the " Favola de Orphio " of Politziano, played at Mantua in 1472. This beautiful poem is somewhat of a tragic nature ; and its main theme, though idyllic, is perhaps too gravely real in tone to be a pure pastoral drama, being a combination of tragedy and pastoral opera. In 1554 Beccari wrote his Arcadian play " Il Sacrifizo ", which was followed by the " Aretusa " of Lollio in

1563, and the "Fortunato" of Argenti in 1567. All thsse, however, were destined to give way before the brilliant and beautiful "Amynta" of Tasso, published in 1573. The Amynta is a poem of transcendent grace, exquisite in expression and unaffected in simplicity. In addition to natural ease and great purity of style, it reveals a charming sympathy with certain phases of nature, which must have deeply influenced the lovers of Tasso in England :—

> " See how creation glows
> In all her works with love's imperious flame !
> Mark yonder doves that bill, and sport, and kiss;
> Hear'st thou the nightingale, as on the bough
> She evermore repeats, " I love, I love";
> The wily snake sheaths her envenomed fang
> And sinuous glides her to her glossy mate :
> The savage tiger feels the potent flame ;
> The grim majestic lion growls his love
> To the resounding forest, Wilder thou
> Than nature's wildest race, spurn'st at that power
> To which all nature bows."*

Tasso was followed by his friend and rival Guarini in his drama " Il Pastor Fido ", acted in Ferrara in 1585. The play has little of the rich and charming imagery of the Amynta, but it has poetry. It is, however, too much bent upon painting a chimerical state of society, to indulge in much appreciation of nature. But both Tasso and Guarini were so popular during the inception of the pastoral in England, that they must have had a considerable influence upon the attitude of the English pastoralists, toward nature.

With the Neapolitan poet, Sanazzaro, the romantic pastoral may be said to have reached its final stage. The work of this poet contains all the pastoral

---

* Amynta, att. 1 sc 1.

elements that had hitherto been striving to blend themselves into one artistic whole. In Sanazzaro the influence of Bocaccio is strong, and there are some healthful traces of friendship with the Syracusan idyls. The poet avows in his introduction, that his object in writing, was to please the jaded imaginations of those who dwelt in cities, by bringing before them the simplicity, peace, and beauty, associated with rural life.

The "Arcadia" of Sanazzaro is a romance instinct with the spirit of poetry, and its rich and easy-flowing periods of musical prose, are interspersed at quick intervals, with passages of exquisite verse. Though most of the characters are too much occupied with their stately wooings to be attracted by mundane things, they are not altogether unconscious of what goes on around them ; and the work throughout breathes an air of genuine appreciation for natural phenomena, and of hearty sympathy with rustic life.

All through the sixteenth century, the influence of Italian romance literature was supreme throughout Europe, and the Italian pastoral was imitated and cultivated in all its forms. This was especially so in England where the master-singers of Italian poetry were widely read, and held in utmost regard. The poets of Spain too, exercised a considerable influence on the pastoral literature of England. During the earlier part of the sixteenth century, the Spanish poet, Joan de la Encina, wrote eclogues, and his fellow-countryman, Montemayor, produced a wonderous pastoral romance, which, with the Arcadia of Sanazzaro, had a very suggestive influence over the English Sir Philip Sidney. Portugese writers, like Falcao and Robiere, gave popularity to the pastoral eclogue in their own country ; and in France Remi Belleau wrote his " Bergeres " in direct imitation of Sanazzaro's Arcadia. The graceful and facile eclogues of Clement Marot, and Amyot's translation of the Greek pastoral, " Daphnis and Chloe " of Longus, also did something to diffuse a taste for pastoral literature in England.

CHAPTER IV

THE ENGLISH PASTORAL BEFORE SPENSER.

WHILE the classical influence of the Renaissance seriously retarded the development of independence and originality in the English mind by stultifying it with too keen a sense of its own inferiority, nevertheless that movement created artistic ideals after which some of the ardent and hopeful spirits did not strive in vain. In England, as on the Continent, the Renaissance gave birth to new forms in literature and other branches of art, and not least among these forms was that of pastoral poetry.

The English pastoral in its form and content, was the direct result of Italian influence, but its evolution was from more various elements than was the Italian pastoral. In England the pastoral was not only of later growth on imitative lines, but it was a product of the classical renaissance combined with a strong native influence, which rendered its idealizing tendency less national ; and from first to last it was rooted in literary tradition rather than in human nature. It stood for some deep longing of the human heart, which the poets were unable to express. A mode of literature, the origin of which was purely academic and artificial, as time went on, naturally lost its hold upon a people whose interests inclined more and more to things of the present, so that poets who were content to contemplate the sun, moon and stars under mythological names grounded on a reality of feeling and faith in legendary gods, became, with the increasing sophistication of the age, merely purveyors of an insipid traditionalism.

We may, perhaps, excuse this aping of classical tradition in the earlier English pastoralists who, under the light of the new learning, were anxious to show their acquaintance with the "Literae Humaniores", but in later poets the cult becomes but a veil to hide the face of nature, and almost everything else that belongs to real life.

The student of literature must not, however, be dissuaded from fruther inquiry into this interesting subject, even if he have to languish at times under the torrid and barren conventionalities of classical tradition or arcadian idealization. It is intolerable, to be sure, to be obliged to face the same landscape and social conditions, whether one is in Britain or Sicily or wandering on the plains of Lombardy, and to be told again and again, that the only beauty in nature is the impossible one of unity without variety. The mediaeval landscape with its moated castle, impregnable walls, well-trimmed gardens and close-cropped hedge-rows, regular angles and lines of trees,—the embodiment of man's handiwork for his own safety, luxury, and social importance, seems to have been the only view of nature enjoyed by poets who pretended to write of country life. At times the only thing that would justify the poet's giving his production the name of pastoral at all, was the slight tinge of the "forest element" that pervaded it; and thus it went on, till at last the very stones cried out in music, and the sweet voices of free nature in woodland bird and murmuring stream, sang down the priests of Pan, and gave to the world a choir more content to hymn the grand harmonies of nature. Yet, strange to say, from out this winter of artifice and convention, arose that literary symmetry and strength that has made possible the consummate art of modern poetry.

In our search after a feeling for nature in the English pastoral, space obliges us to omit the extensive realm of pastoral drama. We all the more regret the restriction, because that phase of its development has much light to throw upon our subject. Although in the pastoral drama, the pressure of human action and emotion is, for the most part, too absorbing to admit of detailed descriptions of nature, it is wonderful how often opportunity is taken for a side glance at some rural scene. Here and there a word in the midst of a dialogue or a song, lets in the open air more refreshingly and tellingly than pages of description.

The pastoral did not at first find in England a very fruitful soil, its growth being slow and disappointing ; and especially at its inception there was scarce an eye to welcome it. English manners were not arcadian nor its climate an eternal spring ; and after the rise of the art lyric, country people seemed to its courtly patrons, ridiculous subjects for poetry. The bucolic muse made her début in so foreign a garb, that the few lovers of English country life, failed to recognise in her a friend, nor even a native of their shores. The country was rich in pastoral life and scenery, and as capable of pastoral idealization as the isles of Greece, but the poets did not turn to nature for their inspiration. Had they been less imitative of the fanciful and flowery Italians, and more sympathetic students of their own rural life and landscape, England might have produced writers like Theocritus and Tasso. But the Italian forms were paramount and the arcadian spirit was in the literary atmosphere of the time ; while the rage for classical idealization was welcomed by the chivalric and courtly classes of Britain.

It is, however, in the Scottish rather than in the English pastoral, that we find the first indication of a genuine sympathy with the feeling for nature, as well as the earliest example of the pastoral itself. No country more easily lends itself to the furtherance of pastoral idealization, than Scotland. Its noble mountain scenery, its well-pastured uplands, the strong moral character and humane domestic life of those who inhabit its vales, all go to make it the natural home of the bucolic muse.

Moreover, the humble existence of the Scottish peasant, affords the pastoral motive possibilities of native sweetness and simplicity, not to be found in English country life. While there is little or no poetry of the English peasantry, the bonnie braes of Scotland have ever been buoyant with snatches of pastoral song. In other ways also, Scotland illustrates the difference between an agricultural and a pastoral people. The Scottish people are more open to those enthusiasms, and tend more to cherish those superstitions, most agreeable to pastoral feeling.. The romantic exultation and healthful out-door life of a people in constant communion with the great and simple forms of nature, free them from the incessant drudgery of the English peasant, and tend so to spiritualize their minds and mysticize their creed, as to foster those emotions natural to pastoral poetry.

The influence of ballad literature, too, was a considerable factor in the evolution of pastoral poetry, on both English and Scottish soil. The ballad was always of the country more than of the town, and it cultivated a feeling for romantic incidents that were drawn out mostly on a rural background. There is in the ballad often a vivid picture of water, and a deep feeling for " haugh and hill ". The fusion of scenery and emotion sometimes goes to illustrate the progress of the story, and to reveal simple and primary feelings for nature. Even the names of persons and places draw the imagination away from urban manners and conventional associations. These old ballads, by way of inuendo at least, condemned the artificial iteration of the drawing-room pastoral, by contrasting it with the simple sincerity of nature, and, like a gulf-stream among the classical icebergs of arcadian fancy, helped to clear the way for the high priests of nature, led by Ramsay, Burns and Wordsworth.

The very earliest appearance of Pastoral verse on British soil, exhibits some evidence of a sympathy with the more beneficent aspects of nature, which we find so conspicuous in later pastorals. About the year 1520 Robert Henryson the " chiefe schole master of Dunfermlyng ", wrote in the ballad form of the French ' pastourelle ', his pastoral dialogue, *Robyn and Makyne*, reversing the order and making the shepherdess (to) woo the shepherd. Its bulk is not large, but it has high merit as revealing a true feeling for nature, and also as poetry. Makyne in vain bestows her attentions upon her rustic love, who at length under the moonlight and the " sweet season ", gives way to her charms, and in turn, solicits, but vainly, her favor, while she, in no manner of the literary pastoral, reminds him that :

" The man that will not when he may,
Shall hauf nocht quhen he wald."

In Henryson we have a poet whose numerous references to nature are introduced with fine aptness, and his portrayal of the characteristic features of his native climate and landscape, is done with a careful and loving hand. " The grasses gracious "—a

delightful aspect of the Scottish hills,—"the pry-
merris and the purpour viola ", give rise in the poet's
mind, to thoughts expressed with great beauty of
language ; and the cold of early spring in the uplands
is pictured in such realistic touches as this :

> " The north wind hud purifyit the air
> And sched the mistie cloudis fra the sky;
> The froist freisit, the blastis bitterly
> Fra pole Artick came quhistling hud and schill,
> And causit me remufe aganis my will ".*

Though William Dunbar (1450–1520) was not a
pastoral poet in the strictest sense of the term, his
influence upon the nature-element in pastoral poetry,
was considerable. Dunbar had a disinterested
delight in the softer side of nature : the notes of birds
and the varied coloring and splendor of the dawn.
He is not quite equal to an appreciation of free, wild
nature, but he has a certain Theocritean delight in
flowers and fields, and sunlit streams, that gives
promise of that pure symbolism of human life and
emotion in the natural world, which reached its
perfection in Wordsworth.

During his later years Alexander Barclay (1475–
1572), another Scottish poet, translated the eclogues
of Mantuan, and though he failed to reproduce anything of the great humanist's charm of style and
imagery, Barclay shows a sincere desire to uphold
rural, as against city, life.

The lack of any sympathetic feeling for the sterner
and grander aspects of nature, such as the sublimity
of mountains and the vastness of sea and sky,
characteristic of the British pastoralists, and poets
generally, may, perhaps, be ascribed to the habit of
associating danger with the unknown. Mountain,

---

* Works, p 75, Laing's Edition.

valley and moor, in those unsettled times, became
symbols of war, robbery, and loss of kindred. The
influence of low-roomed, dark, stone houses in which
winter imprisoned the population, naturally associated the season with misery, causing a shivering wail
for the return of summer. Superstition, also, too often
crudely repressed all æsthetic feeling, so that there
is scant appreciation of art ; and, notwithstanding
the presence of some of the most exquisite ca-
thedrals and abbeys of history, there is not even a
reference to the beauty of architecture. Not until
after the Reformation when the advance in civilization made life easier and less harsh, was sentiment
able to overcome sensation sufficiently to allow the
purer and calmer feelings of men to work free from
the dominating dread and terror of the vast and the
sublime, and to enjoy a spiritual and æsthetic contemplation of nature.

With the publication of Tottell's Miscellany (1557),
collection of poems by various writers, we have the
first faint indication of a real pastoral spirit in English
poetry. The poems are not in themselves pastoral,
but, in the language of Professor Francis Palgrave,
" this volume is the tuning of the instruments before
the symphony opens ". Among much that is refreshingly original in poetry and deeply imbued with the
Elizabethan romance spirit, there are poems by Henry
Howard, Earl of Surrey (1516–1571), which show
an idealized passion interweaving itself with pictures
of rural life,—throwing light on the pastoral of the
succeeding age ; while in the poems of Sir Thomas
Wyatt (1503–1541) we hear the voice of nature
chanting a still more modern music. Indeed, if
Tottell had included in his volume nothing more than
the poems of Wyatt and Surrey, one still could say
with truth :

„ₗThe sonne hath twise brought furth his tender greene,
And clad the earth in lively lustiness."*

Among the more important of the pastoral poets
of this time is Barnabe Googe (1540–1594) whose
Eclogues, Epitaphs and Sonettes appeared in 1563.
Googe shows trace of an intimate acquaintance
with the Italian poets of the age before him, and is,
perhaps, the most elegant of those who essayed the
pastoral before Spenser.   His eclogues are rich in :

" Such tales as winter storms have stayde
In country poet's ryme," †

and reveal a heart open to the moods which seasons
bring.   Googe describes vividly the evils of town
life as compared with the rural parts which he knew,
and laments the decay of the old feudal customs,
following the rise of a cheap, monied, aristocracy :

" I synce I saw such cruel sights,
    dyd never like the towne,
But thought it best to take my sheepe
    and dwell upon the downe." ‡

Again :

" Here in the felds, are pleasant things
    to occupy the brayn,
Behold ! The pleasant hylles adourned
    with dyvers colours fayre,
Give eare to Scilla's lusty songes
    reijoysynge in the ayr ;
What pleasure canst thou more desyre
    than here is for to se." §

It is apparent, however, that Googe's feeling for
nature never rises above the agreeable sensations
derived from outward impressions, with but little
evidence of yearning after the æsthetic and the

---

* Totell's Miscellany, p 3, Arber's English Reprints.
† Eclogue I, 1·15.   ‡ Eclogue III.   § Eclogue VI, p 53

spiritual. Yet he has an eye for the ways of birds,
fishes, and animals, and has glimpses of stars and
sky, that indicate an appreciation of nature for which
we look in vain in some of the more pretensive
pastoralists of the day.

The pastoral mode was now becoming so popular
that those who dared not attempt anything original
in that direction, might at least venture upon a translation, and among the numerous works of this kind
which appeared, we have the eclogues of Mantuan
by George Turberville in 1570. While this volume
is not important save as showing a love for the subject,
containing, as it does, little that is original except a
polish of style and a fine harmony of language, there
are in it a few lyrics, with a pastoral strain of en-
forced sweetness that is not only agreeable, but at
this time very rare.

CHAPTER V

NATURE IN THE SPENSERIAN PASTORAL

WITH the appearance of Edmund Spenser (1552-1599) we reach the turning point of English poetry in general and of pastoral poetry in particular. *The Shepherd's Calendar*, published in 1579, leaves every star of the English pastoral outshone by the sun itself. The genius of Spenser inspired the old pastoral forms with a Chaucerian freshness and a new melody, that made the shepherd a well-understood symbol of lover or poet.

It is an old story that *The Shepherd's Calendar* was bred through foreign inspiration and reared on foreign models, but the poem is much more than the idyllic fancies of Marot, or the arcadian dreams of Sanazzaro. At the Cambridge of Spenser's youth, Petrarch and Bocaccio were in every man's mouth, yet the Italian accent is not inartistically prominent, and the serious and vivacious spirit of Marot lends added inspiration and charm.

Moreover, Spenser's shepherds keep their flocks on the hills of Kent, and his love is a North country lass. The poet idealizes them in the solvent of his own rich imagination, but he does not remove them from their own country or from real life. From the classical and neo-classical tradition and mythology common to the pastoral poets, he freely appropriates what pleases his fancy, but under all, is felt a heart beating in sympathy with every aspect of beauty in nature.

After leaving Cambridge for Lancashire, Spenser met the lady indispensible to all the poets of Petrarch's school, " Rosalynd, the widow's daughter, of the glen ". This fair shepherdess possessed a full share of the cruelty required by all the rules of love

and poetry, which, perhaps, had not a little to do with
keeping the poet's mind drawn to a treatment of
nature in her more active and real aspects. The
main trend of Spenser's thought breaks away from
the conventions of the traditional pastoral, thus
preparing the way for the real English pastoral
wherein the landscape of the eclogue and the pursuits of its personages, have the actual character of
English scenes and peasant life.

In dividing his pastoral into twelve parts called
eclogues, corresponding to the twelve months of the
year, Spenser lays the foundation of his poem on the
background of nature, and shows an insight into the
æsthetic and spiritual symbolism of life around him,
that is quite unique in the pastoral literature of the
time. The summer of his love, dight with daffodils,
apparently is gone, and the unkindly winter's iso-
lation finds relief in hope of change :

‘ You naked trees whose steady leaves are lost,
Wherein the byrds were wont to build their boure,
And now are clothed with mosse and hoary frost,
In-stede of blossomes, wherewith your buds did flouer
    I see your teares that from your boughes doe raine,
    Whose drops in drery yscicles remaine,

And so my lusty leaf is drye and sere,
My timely buds with wayling all are wasted ;
The blossomes which my braunch of youth did beare
With breathed sighs is blown away and blasted ;
    And from mine eyes the drizling teares descend,
    As on your boughes the yscicles depend.'' *

But winter breaks, with the return of the sun from
the south-land :

“ And pleasant Spring appeareth :
The grasse now ‘ginns to be refresh't,
The swallow peeps out of her nest,
And cloudie welkin clereth.''†

---

* March 9—13.   † January 31—42.

Though Spenser's feeling for nature seems often little more than a straining after similitudes, yet it will be found that the inimitable poetry of his verse as frequently owes its excellency to the poet's sincere love of nature as to his charm of language. Many of Spenser's stanzas reveal not only the true poet's absorption in the music of names, but indicate a love of flowers dwelt upon with a Chaucerian element of distilled sweetness even yet more finely rendered :

> " Bring hither the Pinke and purple Cullambine,
>   With gellifloweres ;
> Bring Coronations and Sops-in-wine,
>   Worn of paramoures :
> Strowe me the ground with Daffadoundillies,
> And Cowslips, and Kingcups, and loved lillies :
>   The pretty Pawnce,
>   And the Chevisaunce,
> Shalt watch with the fayre flowre delice ".*

The birds, the first harbingers of spring and the companions of man in sympathy, when all else of life is absent, Spenser loves to praise, delighting especially in the voice of the lark that in summer days "with echoes made the neighbor groves to ring ".† He observes, too, with affectionate minuteness the soaring eagle with his bald scalp, who, as he weened his white head, "a shell-fish down let flye ".

"The goodly oaks "‡ of England, dowered " with leaves engrained in lusty greene,"§ whose acorns "many a swine had larded," Spenser also fondly admires, bringing back to him, as they do, sweet memories of boyhood days among the hills of Kent —days when even in the autumn-tide, all of life seemed spring :

---

* April, 1 : 136. † June, 1 : 52. ‡ February, 1 : 192.
§ February, 1 : 130.

> " I wont to raunge amydde the mazie thickette,
> And gather nuttes to make me Christmas game,
> And joyed oft to chace the trembling prickette,
> Or hunt the hartless hare til she were tame.
>   What recked I of wintrye ages waste ?
>   Tho deemed my spring would ever laste.
>
> How often have I scaled the craggie oke,
> All to dislodge the raven of her nest !
> How have I weried, with many a stroke,
> The stately walnut-tree, the while the rest
>   Under the tree fell all for nuttes at strife !
>   For ylike to me was libertie and life."*

Thus everywhere throughout the pastorals of
Spenser, there is a thrill of buoyant contentment
with nature in her more wild and uncultivated moods,
apart from her beneficent aspects, which indicates,
not only the birth of a new spirit in poetry, but the
presence of a symbolic imagination capable of bringing the conventional pastoral down to something
humane and natural. To Spenser, the varying phases
of nature were but so many voices, each with its
own music :

> " The simple ayr, the gentle warbling wynde,
> So calm, so cool ....,"

and,

> " The grassye ground with daintye daysies dight,
> The bramble bush, where birds of every kynde,
> To waters-fall, their tunes attemper right,"†

and anon the country streams and ancient rivers,—

> " The salt Medway, that trickling stremis
>   Adowne the vales of Kent,
> Till with his elder brother Themis,
>   His brackish waves be meynt,"‡

in these and all other of nature's common things,
Spenser finds an undertone of beauty to the mind
and of solace to the heart.

---

* December 25.-35. † June 25. ‡ July 81.

Although Spenser retains an inkling of the Mediæval dread of the unknown, yet he advances toward an appreciation of the vastness and sublimity of the sea which, to him, is :

" A world of waters heaped up on hie,
Rolling like mountains in wide wildernesse,
Horrible, hedious, roaring with hoarse crie—

*   *   *   *   *

Washing the white feete of Dover Cliffs."

While over the shoreless waste and out of the infinite expanse above, the moonlight plays on " the glittering wave," in contemplation of which, his mind returns to more pleasant things,—the merrymakings of youth in the fields, shaded by cocks of new-mown hay, in company with a maiden of breath " sweeter than the violet," whose voice he loved to hear in the evening, calling her shepherd home to his " curds and clouted cream."

On the whole, the lover of nature will find in Spenser a poet more agreeable than any other pastoralist of the time.   Like Theocritus whom he loved, Spenser brings again upon the pastoral stage, the actual rustics of his native land, speaking their own peasant dialect and living their own lives, yet withal, illumed by the most refined and varied poetry. One is impressed with the belief that the poet must have studied sympathetically the pastoralists before him, and drunk deeply of the common life of the country about him, else he could not have so successfully given unity to previous experiments in pastoral verse, avoiding the artificial manner of the Latin pastoral, and assimilating the emotions of his rustics with the vicissitudes of the seasons, in a manner that does justice both to nature and to poetry.

The pastoral of Spenser has about it an indescrib-
able something that might be termed a haunting
delight in nature, breathing an atmosphere that
is always transparent, sensuous, melodious, dwelling
upon all the fresh and simple elements of life fondly,
through quaint words, fresh scenes, and rejuvenating
tales, rejoicing in love-time and youth which is
always of the morning and the spring.

CHAPTER VI

THE PASTORAL SCHOOL OF SIDNEY

THE decade between the years 1580 and 1590 may be easily designated ' par excellence ' the pastoral period of English song. There is hardly a literary production appearing during that time that does not in some way show a predilection for the pastoral mode.

In the *Arcadia* of Sir Phillip Sidney (1554-1586) published in 1581, we have the culmination of a sentiment that for centuries had been influencing European poetry, and which, more than any other factor, was the means of giving the English pastoral an opposite swing to the movement towards Theocritean simplicity and delight in nature, begun by Spenser. The literary arcadia which arose from the persistent and increasingly exaggerated habit of idealizing the Greek idyls, was· a figment of slow but steady growth. It can scarcely be given a serious place in the idyls of Theocritus. By the time of Virgil the inhabitants of the country have acquired a reputation for music and agile repartee, which only tended to lend credence to the growing fancy that in some way or other the arcadian world, like the name of Sicily, was essentially associated with the genuine pastoral. The fame of Virgil's fourth eclogue, which it became the fashion for pastoralists to imitate, made the term ' arcadia ' identical with the traditional golden age of pastoral innocence,—a note that becomes predominant in the Medieval poets who write in the Latin style after the pastoral manner of Virgil.

This lode-star on the pastoral horizon lured the
eyes of poets away from the face of nature, dazzling
even such writers as Petrarch, Mantuan and Bocaccio, till it finally soared beyond their vision to grace
the more agreeable landscapes of Sanazzaro and
Montemeyor.   These poets had a ˙predominating
influence upon the pastoral mode of Sidney.   Thus
we have the English pastoral in the very glory of
its morning freshness dividing into rival streams :
the one with Sidney to drivel out into the stream of
romance, or vanish into the mists of conventional
insipidity with Pope ; the other with Spenser to
wander over fields alive with the beauty of human
song, growing ever more attuned to visions from
nature's heart and enamoured of her voice, till at
last it becomes a mighty sea of song, its high waves
crested by many a laurel-crowned name, finding
its home ultimately in the sublime depths of Wordsworth and Tennyson.

But to an age whose susceptibilities to the sweet
beauties of nature, were as yet unawakened, the
Italian accents of Sidney were more agreeable
than the rustic songs and field-scenes of Spenser ;
and succeeding poets and romancers in following
Sidney, but reflect the temper of that imitative age.
Sidney followed the poetical landscape of Sanazzaro, but leaned to the complicated love-plots of
Montemeyor, combining so far as he could, the more
artistic elements of both masters with his own
individual note of ideal character-drawing, after
the manner of the chivalric romancers.   The poet is
more intent upon giving expression to the virtues of
the knight than those of the peasant, and is concerned more with events than with nature.   Knightly
deeds are, however, often lighted up by sylvan
scenes and charming impressions, of unique beauty.

The picture of Arcadia, though mainly ideal, displays indirectly some appreciation of nature as she is; and often what seems all too artificial, is but the hand of art making the ideal real. There is to be found here and there a farm among Sidney's parks and gardens of Arcadia. The parks are in the magnificent style of Bacon's essay on gardens; and the description of the "pleazaunt terres of ten foot hy and a twelve brode......with a fresh fine grasse " reminds one of those graceful outlines yet traceable among the ruins at Kenilworth Castle.

The delightful picture of the shepherd boy "piping as though he could never be old," has about it a spirit of immortal freshness more akin to life than anything inherent in arcadian tradition, and was even more exquisitely rendered later by Keats in his *Ode to a Grecian Urn.* The strong personal vein that pervades all the poetry of Sidney, kept him from soaring too far above the haunts of men, and enabled him to throw into his otherwise abstract forms, thoughts on philosophy, and religion, as well as expressions of pure romantic love, that must have had a wholesome influence not only upon the pastoral but upon all the poetry of the time. Moreover, Sidney's complete elimination of all magical and supernatural machinery, after the example of Montemeyor, obliges him to maintain interest in the narrative by curious love-plots in which his own personal character is brought out with great prominence, though even the character-drawing is often as imaginary as any other feature of the arcadian pastoral.

Sidney never forgot that his age was wholly engaged in the contemplation of human affairs. The fashions and amusements of the time were as fantastic and exaggerated as anything appearing in

poetry, and give us some indication of what we are
to expect in the pastoral.   The idealizations of the
latter were mild in comparison with some of the
costumes common to the time ; and the representa-
tions of ladies recumbent on their couches are
obvious reminiscences of the pictures of Tintoretto
and Titian, which Sidney saw in Italy.*

Yet in the midst of his arcadian fancies, and in
an age which had not arisen to any appreciation
of the poetry of the mountains, Sidney could feel
that in some vast inexplicable way, they expressed
a sympathy with his grief :

> " The curteous mountains, grieved at my disgrace,
> Their snowy haire teare off in melting paine." †

And their sublime majesty but reminded him of that
character and mien,

> " Whose beauty shin'd more than the blushing morning,
> Who much did pass in state the stately mountaines,
> In straitness past the cedars of the forest."

The face of nature appealed to Sidney as the face
of beauty incarnate, rather than as a thing merely
æsthetic.   The clouds, like the mountains, have a
voice ; and the moon looking through them, reminds
him of his " moon of poets " :

> " Alas a cloud hath overcast mine eyes,
> And yet I see her shine amid the cloud." ‡

> " O heaven awake, show forth thy stately face ;
> Let not those slumbering clouds thy beauties hide." §

From his sublimal heights Sidney often looks
down upon the face of the earth, and in the voices
of men hears kindred echoes to nature's music ; and

---

* Arcadia, Grosart's Edn, Book iii : p 382.
† Arcadia, Grosart's Edn, Vol. II, p. 45, l. 479
‡   „   „   „   „   „   l. 506
§   „   „   „   „   p. 139, l. 7

he breathes with poetic ecstasy the fragrant breath
of the bean two hundred years before its mention by
Phillips and Thomson : *

> " O words that fall like summer dew on me ;
> O breath more sweet than is the growing beane ;
> O tongue in which all honeyed liquors be ;
> O voyce, that doth the thrush in shrillnesse staine,
>   Doe you say still this is her promise due
>   That she is mine, as I to her am true.
>
> Gay haire, more gay than straw when harvest lies ;
> Lips, red and plump as cherries' ruddie side ;
> Eyes, faire and great, like faire great oxes' eyes ;
> O breast in which two white sheep swell in pride,
>   Joyne you with me, to seal this promise due
>   That she is mime, as I to her am true." †

A gallant knight with many a memory of Chival-
rous Tournament, and of the episodes of gay courts,
could feel and express the esteem in which a fine
steed was held in the society of his time :

> " Have you not seen on some great day,
> Two goodly horses, white and bay,
> Which were so beauteous in their pride,
> You knew not which to choose or ride ? " ‡

Bird life does not seem to appeal to Sidney to
any great degree, but in the humble life of the
pasture and the burrow he finds semblances to
remind him of one,

> " Mild as a lamb ; more dainty than the coney is." §

Or the fronded tops of stately pines, " the cedar
greene of woods," the drops of rain that couple in
hymeneal joy, the fair rocks and goodly rivers, the
vari-coloured flowers blending into one fair vision

---

* Shairp, " The Poetic Interpretation of Nature " p. 199.
† Grosart's Edn, of Sidney, Vol. II. p. 129, " Rurol Poesy."
‡   „   „   „   „   p. 75, l. 15
§   „   „   „   „   p. 8, l. 32

of beauty, of these and a hundred other phases of
nature, Sidney sings with an all but Chaucerian
sweetness; and as evening mellows all the landscape, his eyes wander back to the clouds, beholding
the wondrous interweaving of color that gathers
about the setting sun, and when night's black mantle
falls, walks home with the shepherd, in the small
light of the glow-worm.*

The Sidnian type of pastoral received fresh
impetus from a poet who, though not of the first
class, and chiefly a writer of plays and romances,
yet proved himself a master of pastoral sentiment
in a sweet and delicate lyrical strain.   Robert
Greene (1561-1592), had travelled in Italy, and
there became imbued with the spirit of the native
" Pastoralia ".   Greene appears to have been more
familiar with the ways of the city than of the
country, though his mistaking a Chameleon to be a
bird, may be an unfair test in the case.†   Although
Greene's view of nature forced him into conceits
in order to find something symbolic of his mistress,
—as for example :—

> " Her cheeks like ripen'd lillies steep't in wine,
> Or faire pomegranate kernels washt in milk "—, ‡

yet the sensuous and romantic fervor of his *Menaphon*, and the frequent touches of rustic quality in his
Pandosto, have had no unimportant influence upon
the feeling for nature in poetry.

The arcadian influence of Sidney produced in
Thomas Lodge (1556-1625), one of the most
refined and fervid pastoral lyricists of the age.
Lodge's *Rosalynde* (1590) is an important con-

---

* Grosart's Sidney, Vol. II. p. 153, I 15.
† " Alcida " in Greene's Metamorphosis.
‡ Greene's Works,—Menaphon's Eclogue.

tribution to pastoral drama, and the best model after the masterpiece of Sanazzaro, to be found in literature. It is, however, to his delectable eclogues appended to his epic poem, *Scilla's Metamorphosis* (1587), and to his stray lyrics, that we must turn to find his attitude to nature. He dwells rapturously on many a dreamy woodland scene, "out of space, out of time", where the loves and jousts of an ideal chivalry are tempered by pastoral avocations wherein courteous couples wander amorously through enchanted gardens. Lodge has a keen æsthetic appreciation of nature in her more evident ways, though his feelings at times have to break through artificial conceits and fanciful allusions. With some show of genuine passion he can exclaim :

"Mark how the morne in roseate colour shines!";

and he likes to loiter by the brooks,

"That sweetly float through meades with flowers destrain-
ed,"

and always with an eye for the blossoms by the way : the "milkwhite poppy", and the "tender grasse", concluding with national pride,

"Of all faire flowers, the rose doth sweetest smell."

But for the most part nature is to Lodge not much more than to the other poets of the day, and evidently much less than to Sidney and Spenser. Her apt similitudes flash light for him on life's experiences, and in that lies her chief charm. His lady-love has all the beauty of the winter night :

"Her polished neck of milkwhite snows doth shine
As when the moon in winter night beholds them."

The glory of night is most felt when the moon begins :

"To pierce the veil of silence with her beames."

From the humble life of lowly things he urges needful lessons :

" Learn with the ant in summer to provide,
Drive with the bee the drone from out the hive ;
Byld lyke the swallow in the summer tyde."

Thus in many an inimitable lyric, such as the one beginning; " I turn my looks unto the skies ", Lodge sees in the face of nature beauty and love, and on the whole, there is throughout his exquisite verse a sweet if languid enjoyment in nature, expressed with a delicacy of sentiment that went far to make possible the pastoral tenderness of many a subsequent lyric.

In 1585 Thomas Watson published his *Amyntas*, and in 1592 his *Amyntas Gaudia*, both Latin eclogues, the former of which was translated into English in 1587 by Abraham France. These are, however, quite devoid of any definite appreciation of nature, and are interesting only as showing the trend of the pastoral mode at that time. In 1588 appeared paraphrases of the Theocritean idyls, which though published anonymously, are supposed to have been from the pen of Sir Edward Dyer. John Dickinson in 1592 put forth an eclogue entitled *The Shepherd's Complaint*, which opens with a somewhat harsh burst of hexameters that soften ultimately into a harmonious prose story with lyrical interludes. The year 1598 saw an English version of Montemeyor's *Diana* by Bartholomew Young in which are some traces of the common desire to, see in nature a reflection of life.

CHAPTER VII

MINOR ELIZABETHAN PASTORALISTS

THE atmosphere of Elizabethan poetry was so charged with the spirit of pastoralism that many of the poets who were not strictly worshippers at the shrine of the bucolic Muse, were yet tinctured with her influence, and reveal not a little of her sweetness and charm. Indeed as we survey the names now under consideration it will be at once understood that the term 'minor' can be applied in only a very limited sense to pastoralists whose poetry otherwise not only ranks high in the chorus of Elizabethan song, but whose appreciation of nature's beauty must have been as genuine as it is manifest.

Though the volume entitled *England's Helicon*, was not published until the year 1600, it undoubtedly represents a period carrying us far back into the heart of Elizabethan poetry; and its rich contents make up a garland woven from the choicest blossoms of bucolic song: everywhere is the breath of the springtime, the song of birds, and the joy of youth. The sweet and blissful simplicity of these poems, devoid of all monontonous sophistication and undue brooding upon things sinister, leaves upon the mind a charm that never grows old.

The prevailing spirit of *England's Helicon* appears to be what may be regarded as an æsthetic exhilaration in the glory of fair womanhood whose beauteous virtues are drawn on a background of fields and streams and all of earth's lovely things. It would seem that to man there is no beauty in

nature save that which is capable of suggesting to
him something pertinent of woman. There is but
one answer to the query : What is love ? " It is
December matched with May." " It is sunshine
mixed with rain." And what is beauty ?

> " Beauty sat bathing in a spring,
>   Where fairest shades did hide her ; .
> The winds blew calm, the birds did sing,
>   The cool streams ran beside her." *

The " cherries ripe," † and the fragrant wild
flowers,‡ are but for the lips and lap of love. As
the mother sheep loves her lambs, also the blossom
loves the life-giving sun ; " as the birds do love the
Spring ", so does the poet love his Diaphenia, white
as the sun and fair as the lily.

To most readers of English poetry, the name of
Nicholas Breton (1545-1626) is little known, or
known only as that of some rustic rhymster unworthy
of any serious or extended recognition ; but his
delightful contributions to *England's Helicon,*
and his *Passionate Shepherd* lately edited by
Dr. Grosart, reveal a poet who for more than forty
years had been singing some of the sweetest of
pastoral songs. The easy and elegant simplicity of
Breton, always lighted by a brilliant and fertile fancy,
as well as his homely sympathy with nature,
makes his pastoral lyrics fair fields of delight to the
lover of poetry. The glimpses he gives us of the
old time country-side with its rustic ways and honest
loves, all lightly and languidly thrown off, " with
perhaps too little sense of intellectual effort ", revive
in the nature-lover, memories as gay and rich, and as

---

* " To Colin Clout ", by Anthony Munday.
† " Phillida's Love-call ", by Ignoto.
‡   ,,   ,,   ,,   ,,

tender and pathetic, as Lamb's *Old Familiar. Faces.*

Breton has a quaint but observant eye for the lowly life of woods and fields and an intimate first-hand knowledge concerning the ways of the rural tribes, every recollection of which brings him back to the days of childhood :

> " Who can live in a heart so glad
> As the merry country lad ?
> Who upon a fair green baulk
> May at pleasure sit and walk ?
> And amidst the azure skies
> See the morning sun arise !
> While he hears in every spring
> How the birds do chirp and sing.
> Or before the hounds in cry,
> See the hare go stealing by ;
> Or along the shallow brook
> Angling with a baited hook,
> See the fishes leap and play
> In a blessed sunny day :
> Or to hear the partridge call
> Till she have her covey all :
> Or to see the subtle fox
> How the villain plies the box :
> After feeding on his prey,
> How he closely sneaks away
> Through the hedge and down the furrow
> Till he gets into his burrow.
> Then the bee to gather honey
> And the little black-haired coney
> On a bank or sunny place
> With her fore feet wash her face :
> Are not these worth thousands more
> Than the Courts of kings do know ?
> The true pleasings spirit's sights
> That may breed true love's delights." *

There is in these couplets, a " grace and imagery,"†
and a tenderness of feeling for the every-day aspects

---

* The Third Pastor's Song, Breton's " Worldly Paradise ".
† F. E. Schelling, D. Litt. " Elizabethan Lyrics ", p 226.

of nature, that we do not again find until the days of Ramsay and Burns.

Breton loves to cherish a faith in the old-time fancy of days when little birds did carry tales

> " ' Twixt Susan and her sweeting,
> And all the dainty nightingales
> Did sing at ·lover's meeting;
> Then might you see what looks did pass
> Where shepherds did assemble,
> And where the life of true love was
> When hearts did not dissemble."

The mystic power of woods and fields and changing seasons, weaves a spell about the mind of Breton, more especially in the Autumn days,

> " When the bushes and the trees
> That were so fresh and green,
> Do all their dainty colors leese
> And not a leaf is seen.
> The blackbird and the thrush
> That made the woods to ring,
> With all the rest are now at hush,
> And not a note they sing." *

If the chief glory of Elizabethan literature is the lyric, it is not without significance that some of the finest of these are of the pastoral mode. In the *Passionate Shepherd* of Christopher Marlowe we have one of the most exquisite lyrics in our language. Throughout its chaunting stanzas there is a sweet profusion that bubbles over with woodland music : the notes of birds in Spring and the rhythm of falling water :—

> " Come live with me and be my love
> And we will all the pleasures prove
> That hills and valleys, dales and fields,
> Woods, or steepy mountain yields.

---

* " A sweet Pastoral ".

> And we will sit upon the rocks,
> Seeing the shepherds feed their flocks
> By shallow rivers, to whose falls
> Melodious birds sing madrigals."

These two stanzas from " that smooth song which was made by Kit Marlowe ",* betray a new and charming simplicity superior to the arduous Italian style, and which yet possesses all the rich and versatile imaginative qualities of the poetry of Donne.

The "well-languaged" poet, Samuel Daniel (1557–1592) has left us one or two pastorals which show a ravishing delight in nature as a light set over against the remorse which neglect of honor brings.† Who that has enjoyed the sensation of standing sheltered from an April shower, listening to the chatter of birds just returned from the South, has not caught something of the delectable sociality here set forth in the sweet rhythm and delicate imagery of Daniel's imperishable English ?

> " Now each creature joys the other,
>   Passing happy days and hours ;
> One bird reports unto another,
>   In the fall of silver showers ;
> Whilst the earth, our common mother,
>   Hath her bosom decked with flowers." ‡

The *Affectionate Shepherd* of Richard Barnfield published in 1594, is the work of a juvenile poet, but it takes rank among the finest of English pastorals. Barnfield combines the æsthetic music of Spenser with the classic calm of Jonson, while inclining to the sombre moods of Donne. This young poet facing the darker side of nature, feels the pastoral to be a fit mode for expressing her undertones of melancholy. Though life is blithe and

---

* " Walton's Compleat Angler."
† " A Pastoral."
‡ " An Ode, appended to sonnets of Delia, 1592.

joyous, unvexed by any sorrow that time and song cannot heal, yet in the hush of the woods and pastures is heard the " still sad music of humanity ". All the birds are aglee, save one, and she recalls her rightful name,—

> " Even they did banish moan,
> Save the nightingale alone.
>
>   *   *   *
>
> All thy fellow birds do sing,
> Careless of thy sorrowing."

Even Pan has to suffer and to die. Death is one of the strange spectres that has haunted the pastoral all through its long history, breaking forth at times in those wondrous elegies already mentioned, and venturing faith in the hope that we sow only to reap.

> " The same sweet cry no circling seas can drown
>   In melancholy cadence rose to swell
>   Some dirge of Lycidas or Astrophel,
> When lovely souls and pure before their time,
>   Into the dusk went down." *

So also in Sir Walter Raleigh's pastoral, *A Reply to Marlowe* (1599) there is this reminiscent melancholy which stalks behind all natural delight :

> " The flowers do fade, and wanton fields
> To wayward winter reckoning yields ;
> A honey tongue, a heart of gall,
> Is fancy's Spring, but sorrow's fall.
>
>   *   *   *
>
> But could youth last, and love still breed ;
> Had joys not date, and age no need ;
> . Then these delights my mind might move
> To live with thee and be thy love."

Michael Drayton (1563–1631), one of the greatest of the Spenserians, under the spell of his master's

---

* J. W. MacKail, " Love's Looking Glass," 1891.

music, also chanted many a love-song in the pastoral
mode. The elegant simplicity so essential to bucolic
poetry, was as characteristic of Drayton as of Spenser
himself; and the more finished and interesting of his
poems are decidedly pastoral. His graceful trifles
in language, are at once daring in movement and
felicitous in choice of imagery, triumphantly avoiding
the purely trivial on the one hand and the obviously
burlesque on the other.* The conventionalities of
a pseudo-classicism are not quite absent from Drayton's impressionistic glimpses of landscape, but such
pastoral eclogues as *Nymphidia* sparkle with fantastic tapestries from nature, and have a quick, airy
touch that is instinct with the color and charm of life.

This poet's love is a country lass who lives, as
did Shakespeare's, " far in the country of Arden," †
and could bake biscuit, do needlework, and go to
church on a holyday, as well as yield amorously to
the wooings of a shepherd dressed in a sheep-gray
cloak, till

" She in love-longing fell." ‡

The cheeks of this maiden are like roses and her skin
as snow, and her life is more sweet to him than the
flowers of Spring :

" The verdant meads are seen,
    When she doth view them,
In fresh and brilliant green
    Straight to renew them

And every little grass
    Broad itself spreadeth,
Proud that this bonny lass
    Upon it treadeth ;

---

* " Seventeenth Century Lyrics "—cf. Introductory Essay by
F. E. Schelling D. Litt.
† " Carmen and Dowsabel ", Drayton.
‡   „   „   „   „

> No flower is so sweet
>   In this large cincture,
> But it upon her feet
>   Leaveth some tincture." *

To Drayton each season brings some reminiscence
of what love has meant to him ;

> "For many a long winter's night
>   Have I walked for her."

And with a voice resonant of the glad springtime,
and in an atmosphere redolent of life, he sings of
nature in her free pastoral haunts :

> "The morn no sooner puts her rosy mantle on,
>   But from my quiet lodge I instantly am gone,
> When the melodious birds from every bush and briar
>   Of the wild spacious wastes, make a continuous quire
> The mottled meadows then, new varnish't with the sun
>   Shoot up their spicy sweets upon the winds that run
> In easy ambling gales, and softly seem to pace,
>   That it the longer might their consciousness embrace." †

It is evident from these lines that though Drayton
had the hankering for trim-set gardens characteristic
of his time,—the daisies that damask the lawn, and
the pansy and the violet adorning their odoriferous
beds,— he loved still more deeply the open country,
the wide heath and downs where soft streams
flowed 'twixt lillied banks; and the cliffs and high
hills too where " wholesome winds do blow."   His
also, were the fisher's haunts, dreaming on the
ways of nature along the brooks.   Not only is there
this constant evidence of the piscatorial element, but
moreover of the forest element ; for Drayton was
taken with the grandeur of trees

> " Whose lofty tops do never feel
>   The weight of winter's snows,"

---

* " Sirena "—Drayton Works.
† " Silvius "—   „   „

but whose branches seemed ever alive to a music he ·
always paused to hear :

> " The merle upon her myrtle perch
> There to the mavis sings ;
> Who from the top of some curl'd birch
> Those notes redoubled rings."

And so among the fairy lore of those fascinating
little pastorals of the *Muses Elizium* one might
wander endlessly, yet all the while enchanted by a
voice appreciative of nature.

And here as appropriately as elsewhere we must
call attention to the dear old scholar poet, Thomas
Campion of whose dates we only know that he died
in 1619. In the tiny volume of his verse recently
collected by Mr. A. H. Bullen, there are abundant
evidences of a pastoral appreciation of nature more
gay and winsome than in many of his more famous
contemporaries. This poet, musician, and doctor,
loved the country with a genuine and unsophisticated
passion. To merchant's gold or scholar's fame, he
prefers the nut-brown lass * whose tastes combine
with his for fruit and flowers : her bower is made of
moss, leaves, and willows ; and she loves with him to

> " Trip and skip it o'er the green ; "

and with agile grace and ankles rare, she joins him
in a scheme to

> " Climb up to the apple loft
> And turn the crabs till they be soft." †

Campion admires the free and robust life of the
swain " who can his long flail stoutly toss," with
almost all other things that pertain to rural happen-
ings and environment.

---

* " Amaryllis ".　　　† " Jack and Joan ".

. . Though three of the greatest names contemporaneous with the age under review remain yet to be
considered, they incline so far into the seventeenth
century that we may here fittingly say farewell to
the sixteenth. Standing now at the close of this
wonderous century of song, and looking back along
the bowery arcades of the bucolic Muse, one has to
confess that the British pastoralist even at his best,
seems not yet to have succeeded in rising to that
mental attitude which regards nature as something
admirably æsthetic in itself. For him she expresses
little more than purely human emotions and fancy-
ings. To him nature is a thing to be felt rather
than studied : emotion, not science, is his interpreter.
Fair touches of landscape in hill and copse and
river, the melody of birds and the cooing of men
and maidens, we have in plenty ; but for any deep
appreciation of the real life of men, and the vigorous
voice of nature as expressed in the sublimity of her
mountains, the vastness of her sea and sky, and the
enthralling grandeur of her endlessly varied pano-
ramas, we must wait for a later and more cultivated
time.

Perhaps it is because the pastoral does not easily
lend itself to any profound contemplation of the
more exhalted aspects of nature, that we look in
vain to the sixteenth-century shepherds for any
adequate expression of nature's voice. As in China
and Japan all artistic and poetic conception and
expression are confined to little things—petty pipings
of primitive melodies,— so, though in a vastly more
advanced degree, the Elizabethan pastoralist is
concerned only with those aspects of nature that are
tiny and precise, diminutive and definite ; and if the
knowledge displayed reveals little more than the
acquirements of youth as compared with the subtler

and higher mental grasp of later times, it has nevertheless an unrivalled sweetness; and its fresh and
innocent delight in all natural things will ever
retain a charm for the lovers of true poetry.

CHAPTER VIII

SHAKESPEARE, JONSON, AND DONNE

THE exigency of space that would exclude from consideration all of pastoral import found in dramatic poetry, easily bows to an exception in the presence of the great and " gentle " Shakespeare whose genius was so unable to resist the allurements of the pastoral Muse that in his works are to be found some of the fairest and most unfading flowers of pastoral song. Many of these songs are as gems glowing softly with that quiet descriptive and dramatic element which constitutes the essential quality of all true pastoral poetry ; and withal they reflect a touch of everlasting laughter as sweetly contageous as the rippling melodies of Theocritus.

Born and bred, as his friend, the poet Drayton, remarked, " in the heart of England ", an ideal pastoral environment, Shakespeare had all the gladness and buoyancy of the country boy, as well as that happy sympathy with rural sights and sounds for which the pastoral must ever stand. Those of us who, with bounding pulse and appreciative heart, have solaced all previous desire by treading the haunts of the poet's youth and especially the scenes of his love making, will at once recognize in the lighthearted lyricism of his songs that graceful yet rustic beauty which must have surrounded his early home at Stratford. Whether we stroll over the undulating, varied hills, through whose many a picturesque glimpse of wood and meadow land, the silver Avon flows ; or betimes linger under the

hedgerows and the old, old trees ; whithersoever we
turn, there is the same inevitable impression of what
an eye he had for all he saw in nature.   Every weed
and wild flower laughed to him a song ; the happy
voices of men and maidens in the fields thrilled him
with a lyric impulse ; and even in after years while
buried in the lonely lodgings of dim and dingy
London, there still returned to cheer him the ravishing visions of boyhood, when

> " The winking Mary-buds begin,
> To ope their golden eyes ; "

and also of the

> ...." Daffodils
> That come before the swallow dares, and take
> The winds of March with beauty ; the violets dim,
> But sweeter than the lids of Juno's eyes
> Or Cytherea's breath."

Thus did the "sweet swan of Avon", as Jonson
regarded him, treasure all his memories of gardens,
woods, and fields, as well as seasons and moods, to
give exquisite realization to the fancies and visions
of poetry in those immortal songs over which the
human heart and ear hang with unutterable longing,
because, like the poet himself, they never grow old.

The lyrics of Shakespeare portray the soul and
the imagination of a man who loves to breathe the
free, pure air of the meadows and the open country,
finding at will

> ...." Tongues in trees, books in the running brook
> Sermons in stones, and good in everything "

Lyrics of pastoral suggestion sparkle through his
plays in rich profusion ; and in their airy, æsthetic
fancies, and movement, reflect all the glory of
Elizabethan song.   Indeed it is no small delight to
the lover of bucolic poetry to remember that Shake-

-speare mirrored the most lovely and enduring
charms of Elizabethan song in lines appreciative of
rural life and circumstance. The new delight in
beauty, born in the age of Bacon and Spenser,
became at once the birthright of Shakespeare, and no
extravagance of language or unnatural idealization
among the devotees of contemporary pastoralism,
could dim the divine fire of his own unerring estimate
of

"This blessed plot, this earth............."

which was always to him the best expression of
uplifting, infinite beauty; and hence to be studied
and loved.   He held that not least among the
inspirations of nature, is her capacity for laughter;
and that it also is a part of her strength.   Nor did
his profound acquaintance with the stores of Italian
literature from which he drew the plots of some of
his best plays, tempt him to seek for all fair scenes
under foreign skies; it only served to tincture his
inimitable style with various subtleties and ingenui-
ties that but lend additional charm to his music,
until almost every lyric becomes a chink through
which one catches many a glimpse of the joyous
beauty of the world, and the triumphant heart of
honesty and health.

This great interpreter of humanity sings not so
much of the wealthy, the favored, or any of the
more exclusive circles of human society, but of the
majority,—the common people whom he loved and
of whom he sprang.   The sweet sociality of animate
nature in the open, is the constant source of rural
joy.   The soaring joyousness of the lark, the lonely
notes of the cuckoo, the sinister hooting of the owl,
were all alike to him the songs of this earth, and he
finds in them a music worthy of attention.   The very

humblest creatures escape not his sympathising notice : spotted snakes, thorny hedgehogs, blind worms, weaving spiders, black beetles, and slow snails, are all of some significance in the realm of nature. No brief sketch can adequately convey even a slight idea of the immense range of Shakespeare's appreciation of nature in all her moods and ways, and things.*

He is especially susceptible to the poetic suggestiveness of seasons ; for seasons have their moods, and so have men. Shakespeare found his happiest expression of these in the ever recurring visions of his earlier days. In the exquisite little song on " Winter " from *Love's Labour's Lost* what country boy has not felt the shivering grind of a frosty eventide in January when the pink sun has sunk behind the pines or the snow drifts :

> " When icicles hang by the wall,
> And Dick, the shepherd, blows his nail,
> And Tom bears logs into the hall,
> And milk comes frozen home in pail,
> When blood is nipped, and ways be foul,—
> Then nightly sings the staring owl :
> To-who,
> Tu-whit, to-who,—a merry note,
> While greasy Joan doth keel the pot."

The glad notes of spring and midsummer are in his voice too,

> " When daisies pied, and violets blue,
> And lady-smocks all silver-white,
> And cuckoo buds of yellow hue,
> Do paint the meadows with delight."

But what most solaced the more isolated moments of his unique spirit in this sweet season, were the dreams of former days under umbrageous oaks and

---

* " Fairies' Song " in " Midsummer Night's Dream ".

elms beneath whose spreading beauty he had so
often lain enchanted with the warble of birds, and
the rapture of ineffable emotion.

> " Under the greenwood tree,
> Who loves to lie with me,
> And tune his merry note
> Unto the sweet bird's throat,—
> Come hither, come hither, come hither :
> Here shall we see no enemy
> But winter and rough weather." *

In other songs quite as delightfully responsive to the
echoes of surrounding nature, we perceive through
the pellucid atmosphere of early autumn, premoni-
tions of the sere and yellow leaf.   All her voices
blend and glide in harmonious orchestration.   The
yellow sea sands where the wild waves kiss, the
clarion voice of the cock breaking the fragile silence
of the sleeping morn, the bee still drowsing in the
cowslip's bell, all the glad life of merry summer
reminiscent of goodly harvests and garners never
empty,† all these go to form a realistic background
for Shakespeare's matchless pictures of pastoral life.

Nature has for Shakespeare that same symbolic
and suggestive force that other lovers of the rustic life
have found in her.   The airy beauty of his Sylvia ‡
is like a blossom of the Spring, feasting his eyes
and heart with an ambrosial satiety ; her eyes are
lights that do mislead the morn ; and when faithless,
her breasts are as hills of snow.   That never-to-be-
forgotten picture of the lover and his lass crossing
the green corn field, too overwrought and anxious
with blind, sweet passion to find their way between
the acres of the rye, is like an idyl from some ancient

---

* From " As You Like It ".
† " Marriage Song ", in " The Tempest ".
‡ " Sylvia "—" Two Gentlemen of Verona ".

Grecian vase ; and the murmurous music of cymbals
is heard echoing love's passion in " the Spring time,
the only happy ring time ". Often he hies him over
the dale to the song of the lark

" That tirra lirra chants,"

recalling the ecstatic emotion of other days when to
the notes of the thrush and the jay, he tumbled in
the new mown hay.

If Shakespeare stands for all that there is of
joyous exhilaration and æsthetic idealization in
English pastoral song, his friend and contemporary,
Ben Jonson (1574-1637) represents that classic calm
and contentment which this mode of literature not
less than others, had long been striving to attain on
English soil. The chastely statuesque lyricism of
Jonson, revealing exquisite grace in perfection of
form and beauty of thought, gave edifying impetus
to those who envied his classic sense of moderation,
and emulated his purpose never to account exuber-
ance of fancy equal to high aim. Though Jonson
had a delight in phantasy and those filmy misted
visions that linger along love's intellectual horizon,
he never allowed himself to fall a victim to the
pastoral craze of the time. Its fervor, however, was
past when he became prominent in verse, and it is
more as a force in poetry than as an example of the
shepherd's music, that he here claims our consideration. Jonson was more concerned with the form
than the content of poetry : its perfection of culture
and finish rather than its elaboration of theme. He
it was who could so lift himself above the literary
habits of his time, especially the empirical classicism
characteristic of the Spenserian type with its super-
ficialities of classical allusion and versification, as to
manifest that marvellous quality of assimilative

classicism through which all that is best in the literature of the past may be made to adorn that of to-day, and by which Jonson enjoys the distinction of having exercised a wholesome influence on the form of poetry for all time. In the crucible of his encyclopaedic imagination the poetic virtues of Greece and Rome were transmuted into the more humane and passionate developments of contemporary poetry.

The classical and conservative nature of Jonson, uniting, as it did, all that was chaste and finished in the poetry of the past with all that was most brilliant and accomplished in that of his own age, scrupulously avoided any florrid or extravagant interpretation of the visible world ; it was too much marked by a philosophical and reflective element to sympathize very deeply with the less subjective content of pastoral poetry ; but on its intellectual side it represented an attitude to nature that would have made the pastoral more sane and human, if less rustic. Though Jonson is never caught up into any third heaven by a whirlwind of love, or taken out of himself by the ecstasies of entranced passion, he is always aware of nature, and will not transgress her ways. He was borne on by a single unchanging ideal that there is but one definite and correct way of writing poetry as distinguished from inumerable other ways in which it ought not to be written. To him even the laws of nature need not suffer from the illuminating embellishments of art. Consequently his influence was of a restrictive kind, giving to lyric poetry that perfection of form, and that intellectual and cultured uplift to be noted later in the odes of Milton and Marvell. The foundation of Jonson's poetic intellectualizing is always nature ; his singular fertility of the visual imagination led him often to seize upon a few salient traits through which he endeavored to reflect the truth he wished to convey, as in

> " The lily of a day
> Is fairer far in May," etc.

That Jonson had a genuine appreciation of pastoral nature, and had an eye of sweet and delicate fancy for the haunts of the bucolic Muse, is seen from the fragment he has left us of a play entitled *The Sad Shepherd :*

> " I do not know what their sharp sight may see
> Of late, but I should think it still might be
> As 'twas, an empty age, when on the plains
> The woodmen met the damsels, and the swains,
> The neat-herds, ploughmen and the pipers loud,
> And each did dance, some to the kit or crowd,
> Some to the bag-pipes, some to the tabret mov'd,
> And all did either love or were belov'd."

With the appearance of John Donne (1573–1631) a bolder hand is felt in poetry, and a deeper thrill of passion in its attitude to nature. The melodious sensuousness of Spenser and the romantic meanderings of Sidney, gave way to a more complex music, with some echoes of Bion and Moschus, and prophecies of *Lycidas Thyrsis* the *Adonais* and *Ave Atque Vale.* There is an affectation for the sombre, the obscure, the intricate, accompanied by a brave appeal to the intellect rather than to the feelings, to solve the problem of human happiness, and the relation of man to nature. One has to admit that on these shepherds the smock fits rather awkwardly, and the bucolic theme and imagery are perhaps too often the expression of alien ideas and emotions.

Donne's influence, like that of Jonson, was due more to his unique qualities as a poet, than to his work as a pastoralist; for he has left us but one or two songs set to the music of the pipe. His manner in relation to the form and content of poetry, had a remarkable bearing upon the attitude of poetry to nature in the pastoral sense. Donne's contempt for mere form as such, which led him to discard the poetical apparatus of the past, and made him indifferent to things remote, was compensated for by his exhaltation of poetry to the realm of a new and immense subjectivity : he intellectualizes the emotions to which nature gives rise, and lends himself to beautiful abstractions of light and darkness that dartle like pale pencillings of light through a sombre atmosphere which if often surcharged with amorousness, is none the less frought with spiritual significance.   What Jonson was to the perfection of poetic form and expression, Donne was to the soul of poetry: he was, moreover, an intellectualizing factor of great potency, for without that nameless charm of high poetic thought characteristic of Donne, we could hardly have anticipated poets like Milton and others in that line which reaches its climax in Wordsworth.

One of Donne's pastorals entitled *The Bait*, though claiming to be no more than an imitation of Marlowe's *Passionate Shepherd*, is yet a lyric in which no one can fail to discern a delightfully new and artistic appreciation of nature as the picturesque background against which love silhouettes its rapture and joy. The silver streams with golden strands, like mountain outlines in the pictures of Raphael, stand out suggestively behind the human group ; yet all is infused with love's ethereal passion. It has been held by some critics, with unjustifiable persistency, that Donne's faculty of transfiguring common things with a flood of light opening up strange visions, had much to do with giving the later pastoral and other poetry, that metaphysical trend conspicuous among some of the rustic rhymsters of the decadence.

CHAPTER IX

THE century into which the last chapter has already carried us some little way, but which we must now consider more specifically, was a period of transition in the forms and modes of poetry; and the changes did not always favor a higher development of the pastoral. The Euphuism of Lyly with its poetic prose, admirable for smoothness and charm, made popular the literary use of far-fetched conceits and endless metaphors from classical and other sources; and as it fell in with the fantastic and novelty-loving spirit of the time, it had an influence that was decidedly unwholesome upon a mode of poetry already too prone to extreme idealization and extravagant device. The fine imaginative qualities of Dean Donne and the calm and cultured atmosphere of Ben Jonson did not succeed in lending spontaneity to the lifeless classicism of Waller; and the drift toward mere conventionality maintained a steady and increasing influence until by the middle of the seventeenth century, there was in poetry a complete change of subject and of treatment.

As this movement was in the direction of the precise in form and the abstract in thought, abounding in a vague generality of sentiment, the poets were further than ever removed from a genuine appreciation of nature for her own sake; so that naturally the pastoral in time fell to a tarnished name. Most of the poets now abandoned the wild woods and the open generally, for the stately and mechanical circuits around the box-walls of a labyrinth.*   Instead of the direct appeal to nature and the naming of specific objects, they substituted generalities and second hand allusions.   This substitution of the general for the particular, and of periphrastic locution for direct speech, ultimately left the pastoral Muse a lifeless statue pedestalled in the artificial gardens of Twickenham, its disembodied spirit wandering unclothed until it found a welcome re-incarnation in the gentle shepherd of the Caledonian hills, and permanently later with the great high priest of nature, amid the Cumbrian dales. Thus the formal pastoral of tradition ultimately gave way before the demand for a greater naturalism and a closer fidelity to observed truth.

It would be a mistake, however, to be hypercritically tempted into regarding the Seventeenth Century as a period in which there were no great poets, or even few sincere pastoralists.   Indeed some of the greatest names of literature grace the pages of its history ; but from the brilliant choir of lyricists that usher in the century we might well feel justified in having expected a more vivid and vital appreciation of nature than the age manifested. There is in the whole history of literature no such well sustained volume of lyric utterance as the closing years of the Sixteenth Century produced, and almost every singer has caught something of the pastoral sweetness ; but the acclaim with which the succeeding century received that matchless burst of song, soon lost its fervor, and the age began to give signs of the petrifaction that was settling down upon the society of the time : hence the brilliant display of meteors began to fall, and as the century filtered out, but few of them hung fire.

---

* *E. Gosse :* " From Shakspeare to Pope," P. 9.

In the modest and unassuming poet, William Browne (1591–1645) nature found a pastoralist after her own heart; for with Browne came a wealth of country imagery and similitude unknown to the average Seventeenth Century pastoral.   He does not‘ perhaps, rise to so serene a height of the symbolic imagination as Herrick, but nature is to him sufficiently spiritual and human to leave some consciousness of her æsthetic and beneficent aspects.

This poet loves to dream of delightful groves perfumed with

“ Oderiferous buds and herbs of price ”,

where fruits hang in luscious clusters, and birds tune their notes to the music of running water,—a scene so fair

“ That you are fain
Where last you walked to walk again.”

Though Browne could not find this Sicilian arbor in his native Britain, he discovered the nearest suggestion to it that his country could afford ; and there in his tiny village by the Devon sea, he sweetly sang of it his long life through.   Unperturbed by the restless activity that inspired, especially the dramatic poetry of his time, he was all for pastoral contentment, grateful for the fragrance that nature exhaled, and cheered by the breezes that blew down her leafy alleys.   He softly sings of family circles and village groups footing the green to the music of the shepherd’s pipe, all under the shade of pleasant summer leafage : of rustic bridals and junketings ; of fishing, chasing the squirrel, and gathering the nuts, with a joy sustained and uncloying, and withal out of a heart exempt jrom old age.   Notwithstanding the contempo-

raneous temptation to indulge in far-fetched conceits
and recondite allusions, Browne delights more in
the simple and homely images of rustic environment:

> " My muse for lofty pitches shall not roam
> But homely pipen of her native home ; "*

and thus again of his own Devonshire he felicitously
sings, giving adequate appreciation to one of the
most charming of English landscapes :

> " Hail thou my native soil ! thou blessed spot
> Whose equal all the world affordeth not !
> Show me who can so many crystal rills.
> Such sweet clothed valleys and aspiring hills,
> Such wood-ground, pastures, quarries, wealthy mines,
> Such rocks in which the diamond fairly shines."

Nor does he forget those

> ... ..." homely towns
> Sweetly environed with the daisied downs "

from whose fair hedgerows

> " Doth spring the queen of flowers, the English rose."

The melodious glory of a summer morning had
sweet enthrallment for this poet of the fields :

> "..........See the spring
> Is the earth's enamelling,
> And the birds on every tree
> Greet this morn with melody :
> Hark how yonder thrustle chaunts it.
> And her mate as fondly vaunts it.
> See how every stream is dress'd
> By her margin with the best
> Of Flora's gifts ; she seems glad
> For such brooks such flowers she had.
> All the trees are quaintly 'tired
> With green buds, of all desired ;
> And the hawthorn every day
> Spreads some little show of May :
> See the primrose sweetly set

---

* Britania's Pastorals: Bk I, Song 1. l. 13.

> By the much loved violet ;
> All the banks do sweetly cover,
> As they would invite a lover
> With his lass to see their dressing
> And to grace them by their pressing." *

As the glory of a long calm summer day is over, who has not caught the scent of fields at sunset ?

> " The fertile meadows with their pleasing smells,
> The woods delightful and the scattered groves," †

earth's best odors aromatical, that exhale especially from

> " Within the field which long unploughed lies, ‡
> Somewhat before the setting of the sun."

And then with what accuracy he observes how

> " The sable mantle of the silent night
> . Shuts from the world the ever-joyous light."§

But to him as to other poets, the passing of summer days, brings the pain that clings to all desire, and with the autumn,

> "..........birds cease their notes,
> And stately forests don their yellow coats,
> When Ceres' golden locks are nearly shorn
> And mellow fruit from trees are roughly torn."

Browne often dwells fondly upon the appearances of sky and sea, more especially " the rainbow's many coloured hue " blending to a unity symbolic of the beauty of life, like to the changes which we daily see about the " dove's neck". He views nature as something in sympathy with man whom no one season or color can fully satisfy ; neither

---

* The Shepherd's Pipe, Eclogue I : l. 2.
† Britania's Pastorals, Bk. II : Sny 4, l. 22.
‡ Britania's Pastorals Bk. II. Sny 4. l. 571,
§   "   "   "   "   " 3. l. 1000,

"Summer, Autumn, Winter, Spring,
Nor the best flower that doth on earth appear
Could by itself content us all the year.
The salmons, and some more as well as they,
Now love the freshet and then love the sea ;
The flitting fowls not in one coast do tarry,
But with the year their habitation vary." *

This poet evinces a close and tender observation of nature in her endless aspects, the whispering gale that dallies with the leaves along the dale; " the jocund spring wherein the leaves, to birds' sweet carolling, dance with the wind ;" the ravine between the hills " like the gliding of a snake desending," all hushed and silent as the wind of night; and above all else, the flowers, each of which he mentions with praise, even to

" The daisy scattered on each mead and down,—
A golden tuft within a silver crown." *

He also dwells with an element amounting to ecstasy at times, upon the symbolic qualities of the forest trees, including

" The oak that best endures the thunder shocks "

and

" The fir that oftentimes doth resin drop."

He loves to wander betimes by the river that dashes down the rocks, and then creeps away, worming its course through the meadows. Much of his life was spent near the " unsatiate everthirsty sea ", often loitering on its shell-strewn shores, watching the children revel on the sands.

Browne's most distinctive notes are those of landscape, with abundance of sweet country air and summer weather, upon which he dwells with a tender arcadian simplicity. From the narrow limits

---

* Britania's Pastorals, Book II : 3, 1, 351.

of his hamlet at Tavistock, he was able to catch
every note that hill and dale give forth, and his
descriptions of sunrise and sunset have always a
quaint and unapproachable charm.

The amazing literary fecundity of George Wither,
the friend and great admirer of Browne, resulted in
little that is appreciable in poetry, but the most
important of what he wrote is in the pastoral strain,
and with plenty of rusticity and honest country
sense.   However, amid a good deal of fluidity and
flatness, we sometimes find a stray lyric of immortal
freshness and charm.

Wither's mistake in expressing too freely some
of his political opinions, resulted in his spending a
considerable portion of his life in prison where he
relieved his heavier moments by perusing the
pastorals of his friend Browne, which brightened
many an hour of his grim confinement by bringing
back to him memories of the happy days of
childhood in the country where,

> " Each morn as soon as daylight did appear
> With nature's music birds did charm the air." *

Again he breaks out,—

> " I miss the flowering fields
> With those sweets the springtime yields."†

Wither was especially charmed by the song of birds,

> " The heavenly music of the rural plain",

and included among his songsters even the ravens
that

> " Croak their black augeries from some black wood."

But he seems to have been most at home in the

---

* Geo. Wither " Shepherd's Hunting, Eclogue 3, l. 230
† "   „   „   „   „   4, l. 345 and 375

expansive fields, wandering about in homespun gray, reclining at times under the shade of beechy groves :—

> " See if any palace yields
> Ought more glorious than the fields."

Of nature he declares :

> " By a shady bush or tree
> She could more inspire in me
> Than all nature's beauties can
> In some other wiser man."†

Phineas Fletcher (1582–1648) though one of the minor Spenserians, proved himself no less appreciative of pastoral themes than his great master ; and in his more natural and felicitous moments, Fletcher gives forth rare echoes of Spenser's luxurious sweetness. Fletcher's variation from the ordinary pastoral νοήματα shows that to some extent he was influenced by the writings of Sanazzaro, if not also by those of his contemporary Drayton, both of whom were much disposed to similar piscatory rambles ; but Fletcher's fishermen are English, haunting the Thames and the Cam rather than the vague open sea. These people of the streams are genuine pastoral characters such as Theocritus loved. In the alembic of the poet's imagination they are made to breathe the fresh free air of running waters, and to feel the exhilaration of contentment appropriate to pastoral verse. Love is their refreshment under every oppressing monotony of existence ; and all nature is its symbol. Woman's face is like the May, and her eyes may be compared unto the sun ; her " brown and shady hair " is soft as night to tired eyes, and portends " sweet rest and gentle ease."*

---

* Eclogne VII ; " Thomalin."
† Shepherd's Hunting, Eclogue 4 : l 375

William Drummond of Hawthornden (1585–1649)
has one or two pastoral sketches in verse, in which
the unfeigned love of nature is so lucidly immanent
that we cannot forbear to mention them, though
they do not appear to express adequately the sweet
passion of the poet's mind.   Nature's voice is there,
but the ear detects only her muffled tones threat-
ening to break forth, like music from a hurrying
brook, or from the hush of lofty pines : it is a music
suggested rather than expressed, leaving in the mind
a consciousness of some remembered sweetness.

Drummond lived secludedly amid the fresh charms
of a romantic dell fragrant with the scent of
hawthorn blossoms, and through which the Esk
winds its slender way past Roslin castle ; but he
does not make this enthralling environment a direct
matter of poesy.   He was too much haunted with
visions of a departed happiness, ever sighing, as did
the poet of a later time :

> " Oh for the touch of a vanished hand,
> And the sound of a voice that is still ! "

To Drummond nature was a fond assistant and com-
panion in his life-long search for that lost love ; and
so from his tersely expressed sentiments in lines of
much-conscious sweetness, we are sensible of little
more than the odor of " musked eglantines", the
notes of birds among the statuary of his phenomenal
garden, and withal a conscious presence of the sweet
hermitress whose loss he never ceased to deplore.

Drummond's landscape is too generalized to allow
of the lovely scenery of Hawthornden finding any
very distinctive place in it.   But the poet's heart is
soundly loyal to nature ; and the manifest tokens of
Sidney's grace, and the deep Elizabethan charm,
characteristic of his verse, link Drummond not only

with the pastoral poets of the past, but with the true nature-lovers of all time.

Among the poets redolent of rural sweets Robert Herrick (1591–1674) easily takes a position of undisputed prominence, and indeed may be looked upon as the laureate of pastoral England. He has been regarded by some as the poet's pastoralist : " an Ariel of poets, sucking where the bee sucks, from the rose heart of nature and reproducing the fragrance idealized."*

Herrick's verse is odorous of new mown hay ; all things have on them a morning light : long shadows streak the grass, and the dew lies white and brilliant upon the leaves, while out of the shimmering distance comes the shrill yet silver sound of whetting scythes, and the merry laughter of youths and maidens.

In the eyes of this poet all nature is as love in blossom. One chord pervades his poetry, one heart-song in praise of idealized love of whose every charm nature is the constant similitude. Her cheeks are " like cream enclareted ", and her " eyes like purest skies ". An aroma breathes about her like the essence of jessamine, and the " smell of morning milk and cream "; the breath of kine and sheep is sweetened by her presence, and where she goes,

" How each thing smells divinely redolent,
Like a field of beans when newly blown,
Or like a meadow being lately mown.† "

To the poet, love comes as mysteriously

" As colors steal into the pear and plum.‡ "

---

* E. B. Browning ; " Book of the Poets."
† Hesperides No. 422.   ‡ Hesperides No. 739.

The pastoral, *Corinna Going Maying*, is recognized as one of the most perfect studies of idealized village life in poetry. "In this poem Herrick has invented a new and dainty pastoral mode of his own by a fresh return to nature.* " Herrick is in revolt against the fashionable conventionalities ruling in contemporary poetry, complaining that the spirit of the pastoral has forsaken the hills and vales,

> " And for a rural roundelay
>   Strik'st now a courtly strain ."†

The little poem, *To Phyllis*, is a pastoral lyric equal in sweetness to Harlowe's *Passionate Shepherd*. *Oberon's Feast* reveals a poetic insight gifted by a sweep of language seldom rivalled in poetry, the whole being characterized by a sympathy with the humble life of nature, that is exquisitely tender and human. The king of the fairies makes a toothsome meal on

> " A moon-parched grain of purest wheat ",

and has the

> "........chirring grasshopper,
> The merry cricket, the puling fly,
> The piping gnat, for minstrelsy."

To quench the royal thirst,

> " A pure seed-pearl of infant dew
> Brought and besweetened in a blue
> And fragrant violet.........."

is sufficient. Herrick lived most of his life in a country parsonage, and when not writing, loved to wander in the fields, especially in the spring when

---

* F. E. Schelling, D. Litt.—"Seventeenth Century Lyrics ".
† Hesperides, No. 494.

" In green meadows sits eternal May ",*

and all nature is

" Reclothed in fresh and verdant diaper."†

In the early hours of day,

" When the cock (the ploughman's horn)
Calls forth the lily-wristed morn ",‡

and the breeze scarcely stirs the nodding leaves of trees, the poet was accustomed to sally forth alone to see

" The morning sunshine tinselling the dew ".

Amid Herrick's light and sensuous descriptions of the gay and beautiful side of nature, there is here and there a touch of amiable melancholy; in the daisies that close too early in the " dull eyed night ", and in the " grove tinselled with twilight ", he beholds symbols of the passing glory of the world. Though he mentions all the flowers, and with a feeling seldom less than passionate, yet they but remind him of the uncertainty of all sweet things, and the ideal love above his grasp :—

" For as these flowers thy joy must die,
And in the turning of an eye ;
And all thy hopes of her must wither
Like those short sweets ere knit together ".§

Herrick is, moreover, never unconscious of the higher symbolism of nature, and often turns from the fond familiarity of common things, to roll yearning eyes upward to the source of all true love and beauty :

---

* Hesperides No. 577. † Hesperides No, 644. ‡ Hesperides No. 664.
§ " A sweet Pastoral ".

> " Thou see'st a present God-like power
> Imprinted in each herb and flower ".

John Milton's (1596-1674) great epics and odes
are strewn here and there with idyllic scenes and
pastoral elements that indicate an appreciation on
the part of the great poet for the arcadian aspect of
nature.   Into the swinging lines of his narrative or
the effusion of his passion he brings the restful
sweetness of many an uninvited note from the
bucolic pipe :—

> ".........Return Sicilian muse,
> And all the vales, and bid them hither cast
> Their bells and flowerets of a thousand hues ".

In *Comus, Orcades*, and *L'Allegro* there is abundant evidence of a pastoral feeling for nature, though
it is more or less subservient to the classical influence
then becoming prominent in poetry.   The hereditary
" enamelled green " which Dante saw in Purgatory,
but which has never been seen anywhere else,
though affected by many poets never vouchsafed
the Dantean vision, Milton also admires, yet he has
at least an equal eye for the " muskrose of the
dale ", and loves, as who would not, the delicious
scent of honeysuckle banks.   Milton's consummate
art as a poet did not render him proof against the
habit of his time in resorting to indirect speech ;
hence he is often more deeply moved by the " savory
herb " than by the green grass itself, but for all
this he adequately atones by his love of " twilight
meadows " and country streams, still peopled for
him with the mysterious beings of classic poetry :

> " Sebrina fair
>   Listen where thou art sitting
> Underneath the glassy, cool translucent wave,
>   In twisted braids of lillies knitting
> The loose train of thy amber dropping hair ;
>   Listen for dear honor's sake,

Goddess of the silver lake,
Listen and save."

In Lycidas we behold all nature made to weep, which is the last note of that sweet mournfulness characteristic of the old Spenserian time, and now passing irrevocably out of poetry.

In the poet Andrew Marvell (1621-1678) we may take a fitting farewell to the pastoralism of the seventeenth century; for in his fine imaginative intensity fusing together thought and feeling in regard to delight in nature, there is an appreciation of pastoral environment even greater than that of the Elizabethan poets, and withal a premonition of the natural school which was to find its crown in Wordsworth.

Marvell's view of nature is at once sharply removed from that of the other pastoralists of the time. He withdraws from the rollicking mirthfulness and gay objective contemplation of his contemporaries and assumes a keenly intellectual and introspective attitude, mingling his narrative and description with a degree of reflective passion not fully developed until we reach the poet of Grasmere. Marvell's manner is as dignified and as solemn as that of his friend Milton, yet not without a light and triumphant grace that resembles George Herbert, and a sparkling intellectuality that foretells Shelley. Through the scintillae of his imaginative hyperbole we catch many a sweet and delicate fancy exquisitely wrought, as, for example, in the young girl's description of her fawn, " whiter than milk " and that, living among the lilies and eating roses, was all

" Lilies without and roses within. "

Marvell does not, therefore, wholly succumb to the anomaly of a supremely subjective pastoral mode; his ardent love of nature found rest and refreshment in her color and beauty, and sufficiently softened the glare of a cold intellectuality, to reveal a poet sweetly sensitive to the lilt of birds, and the texture of blossoms, with plentiful echoes of receding Elizabethan song. His imagination is alive to the notes of the nightingale chanting to the living lamps of the glow worm ; and he joins in the ejaculatory catches of the mower in his meadows fresh and gay. And often beneath Marvell's rather fanciful artificialities, are found a wealth of descriptive charm and artistic skill not unworthy of his master Horace, though with plentiful music of a more modern tone.

This gentle poet especially loved the fair quiet of garden haunts where nature has her more modest ways ; he was prone to linger down the orchard paths where ripe fruit drops by the mossy roots of trees. Marvell's poem entitled *The Garden*, is a charming example of what a fine nature lyric should be : it reveals the suggestive power of natural objects to stimulate the imagination, some consciousness of which is manifest in the apt couplet:

> " Annihilating all that's made
> To a green thought in a green shade. "

Marvell would avoid the society of those who love

> " To sport with Amaryllis in the shade
> Or with the tangles of Neaera's hair ;"

for he prefers to contemplate nature with all the high seriousness of Milton's muse. Though he was undoubtedly impressed with the outward beauty of things in nature, he is perpetually haunted with Puritanical suspicions of her malignancy, especially in affording undue encouragement to the play of primitive passions and conniving at the chaos of undeveloped conditions. Thus he admits that the cave is love's shrine, but warns that it is virtue's grave, a cautious didacticism not always character-

istic of pastoral ethics. This pastoralist would lift
up his eyes unto the hills, and yield himself
constantly to the wholesome spell of skyey influences. In the endless nebulosity of the milky-
way, he beholds the symbol of everlasting day, for
his Arcadia is beyond the realm of finite things. It
is to Marvell's description of "Elysium" that Shelley turns for suggestion in his "Queen Mab".

Doubtless this poet's fear of the world may in
some measure be ascribed to the spirit of his age;
his was an era of treachery and revolution, and the
fair land was over-run with treason and besprent
with human blood. And if in nature's myriad faces
men see but what they are, it may well be that the
poet hears in her orchestra echoes of those griefs
and fears that press in upon him from without.
Thus lured to a poetic contemplation of the beautiful
yet lustful earth, made still more despicable by the
horrors of war and the hate of partizan strife, the
poet sees many a pessimistic aspect : sorrows that
cut like a scythe ; hopes that whither like grass ;*
loves so fair, yet thistle-like. To him as to the
Japanese poet, the most conspicuous creatures of
humble life, are the frogs wading in the pools, the
snake glittering in his second skin, the grasshopper
hiding in the shade, and the everchanging chameleon.
Through the sombre atmosphere of his erruptive age
and above the narrow religious influences that were
his, he portrays a pastoral landscape that shows his
passion for nature undulled and serene; beneath his
mask of care there is a love of flowers and trees, and
a longing for outdoor life, that are quite delightful.
Marvell's rich imagery glows with genuine pictures
from nature; and his music is like the gurgling of
a brook gleaming its way under the leafage.

* "Damon and the Mother."

CHAPTER X

NATURE IN THE EIGHTEENTH CENTURY PASTORAL

IT is extemely difficult to characterize the feeling
for nature in the pastoral poetry of the
eighteenth century. It was an age of bold
experiment and spontaneous transition with vast
contemporaneous differences between poets and
poetry. There is, moreover, a strange overlapping
of movements in literature, which tends to baffle
any precise analysis of motives in regard to the
feeling for nature.

To many students the prevailing movement of
the century was that represented by Pope and
carried by his followers to exhaustion,—a movement
wherein the country becomes a playground for the
educated and courtly classes whose only appreciation
of nature appears to be inspired by cold and critical
imitations of classical tradition, clothed in the
language of insipid conventionality.

But on the other hand there was a distinct and
influential movement toward nature and man, which
under the genius of Thomson and Ramsay, brought
into poetry, not only a more fervid feeling for rural
scenes, but some of the color, fragrance, and music
that "golden tongued Romance with serene lute,"
longed to welcome. The prevailing drift of the
age, however, was utilitarian in thought and therefore materialistic in its conception of nature ; and no
poetry, least of all pastoral poetry, could withstand
the blighting anonymity of a loveless age. The
England of fresh and verdant pastures spotted with
recumbent cattle,—with its landscape of long deep

lanes and quaint hamlets,—had given way to the
England of congested cities and world supplying
manufactures.   Such a population gladly substituted
for the arcadia of the pastoralists, the more demo-
cratic consideration of well-cultivated fields feeding
the hungry millions of the world.   The merchant-
princes of London had but scant respect for poetic
idealization, and regarded the country more as a
source of food-supply than as a subject for poetry.

In full sympathy with this luxurious era of the
new-rich, was its most typical poet, Alexander Pope
(1688–1744).   Pope's pastorals were published in
1709, and were considered by some of his contemporaries a charmingly natural presentation of country
life.   But to genuine critics like Warton and others,
their most salient characteristic was a slavish
imitation of classical tradition ; and though, for this
reason, few writings have met with harsher or more
fastidious criticism, the judgment of subsequent
critics has varied but little from that of the Wartons.
Pope did not professedly aim at originality, but
claimed to have imitated the great masters of the
ancient eclogue ; and the gleanings from Virgil
especially, as Dr. Johnson remarked, were " ambi-
tiously frequent ".   But while we are tempted to
infer that Pope's references to nature are no more
than the reflected enthusiasm of Virgil, it may be
safely suspected that the poet had a warmer
sympathy for nature than the narrowness of his
Latin mould permitted him to express, for many
a remark here and there escapes him, hinting the
presence of a love for Spenser which the limitations
of tradition obliged him to suppress.

A conspicuous example of the closeness with which
Pope followed his master, may be seen by comparing

the view of nature shown in the following lines from
the pastoral on " Spring " :—

> " Then sing by turns, by turns the muses sing;
> Now hawthorns blossom, now the daisies spring ;
> Now leaves the trees, and flowers adorn the ground.
> Begin : the vales shall every note rebound ".—,

with Virgil's third eclogue, line 59 :—

> " Alternis dicetis ; amant alterna Camoenae
> Et nunc omnis ager, nunc omnis parturit arbos
> Nunc frondent Sylvae, nunc formosissimus annus ".

It is of course difficult to assume the sincerity
of a poet who in the eighteenth century undertakes
to describe the processes of nature in terms of
mythology ; mythological influences which were
earnest guesses at truth on the part of Virgil become
the very tamest of conceits when taken as prototypes
for the age of Pope.   The changes of the seasons
Pope ascribes to the presence or absence of the
nymphs whom his minstrels celebrate.   In Spring
the flowers will not bloom nor the birds sing until
Delia smiles.   In Summer the breezes await the
movements of this heroine ; and in Autumn the
leaves fade and the flowers wither because she has
departed.   In Winter all is cold and lifeless because
Daphne is dead.   In these archaic fancies our fathers
affected to find a poetry of nature, but if poetry is,
as Wordsworth avers, " The image of man and
nature ", then Pope's view of nature is, to say the
least, non-poetic, for it is an image of neither.

And so one finds in Pope many a line which
though singularly sweet in versification, is altogether
too artificial as a poetic conception of nature :

> " Ye gentle muses leave your chrystal spring,
> Let nymphs and sylvans Cyprus garlands bring.
> Ye weeping loves the streams with myrtles hide,
> And break your bows as when Adonis died ;

And with your golden darts now useless grown,
Inscribe a verse on this relenting stone :
Let nature change, let heaven and earth deplore,
Fair Daphne's dead, and love is now no more."

This transcription partly from Virgil, and partly
from Ovid who drew his picture from Bion's first
idyl where the loves break their bows in paroxysms
of grief over the death of a loved one, becomes
meaningless on the lips of one whose loves snap
their bows not because of uncontrollable sorrow,
but at his instigation, and for the sake of one whom
the poet had never seen.

Pope's poem on *Windsor Forest* is, as Professor Courthope asserts, "the first professed
composition on local scenery since Denham and
Maryell". Wordsworth professed to have seen in
it " a passage or two " containing new images from
external nature, but the poem is on the whole so
vague that its definite references would apply
equally well to places outside of Windsor Forest.
There is, however, some exact observation, though
devoid of feeling,—in reference to the doves flocking
to the trees, the flight of the clamorous lapwing,
the trembling trees reflected in the stream, and
to the purple heather of the hills,—which is hardly
adequate to atone for the poet's general insensibility
to the subtle and latent beauties so obvious in nature,
to the practiced eye. In the pastorals of Pope, as
in most of the poetry of the time, the indications of
a genuine love for nature are fugitive, occasional,
and unconscious, yet underneath all this insipidity,
a change from the formal to the natural school
was going on, and in poets like Ambrose Phillips,
Gay and Ramsay, we see the artificial shepherds
and shepherdesses of the conventional pastoral
being supplanted by something more true to life.

Contemporaneously with Pope, Ambrose Phillips (1671–1749) undertook to revive an interest in pastoral poetry by writing after the manner of Theocritus, Virgil, and Spenser.   Phillips is a close imitator of Virgil, even to the extent of introducing animals never seen in England.   He also represents the English climate as producing the lily, daffodil, and rose at the same season, which drew upon him the satire of Pope.   But notwithstanding his errors and anachronisms, Phillips has a keen regard for the pleasing features of landscape, and evinces a closer friendship for nature generally, than any of his immediate predecessors in the pastoral mode. Even through his classical immitations there shine out at times some surprising and pleasant first-hand observations of true and charming aspects of nature, drawn entirely from country life.

There is a quiet touch of color in those lines, which leaves upon the mind a sense of restfulness like the shade of summer afternoons :—

" This place may seem for shepherds leisure made.
So close these elms inweave their lofty shade
The turning woodbine how it climbs to breathe
Refreshing sweets around on all beneath ;
The ground with grass a cheerful green be-spread,
Through which the springing flower uprears its head."

Phillips apparently finds no allurement in mountains and waterfalls, nor in the hills where the shepherds were wont to roam and watch the silent rapture of their flocks :—

" The rocks and floods pour forth a ceaseless moan ",—

but for animate nature his heart is more open :—

" And now the moon begins in clouds to rise,
The brightening stars increase within the skies,
The winds are hushed, the dews distil, and sleep
Hath closed the eyelids of the wearying sheep ".

The song of birds had for Phillips a music of its
own, and he refers with poetic fervor to the sportive
chase of the swallows, the note of the cuckoo, and
the speckled breast of the thrush. His poetic fancy
is also stirred by the fleeting dusky shadows of the
fields cast by the moving clouds, the blue color of
the mists, the sweet odors of the morning, and the
moaning of the night winds among the trees. For
the most part, however, nature is to Phillips but the
idyllic background on which to portray the emotions
of some pastoral nymph or swain ; some Rosalind
whom he loves to amorously praise by heaping up
images from nature.

In the burlesque pastorals of John Gay (1685–
1732) there appears a deeper appreciation of nature
than in Pope or Phillips, or indeed any of those
polished contemporaries who laughed at his rugged
verse. Gay's *Shepherd's Week* was intended as
a parody on the pastorals of Phillips, but in this
poem the author achieved the distinction of having
invented a new form of literature,—the Comic
Opera ; and the man who brought forth this time-
enduring mould in which so much of Anglo-Saxon
humor has been cast, deserves the homage which
the history of literature accords him.

Though the pastorals of Gay are by no means of
of the first order of poetry, they were the first real
attempt since the time of Elizabeth, to throw aside
the classical tradition of nymphs and swains, and
return to the naturalness and simplicity of Theocritus.
This rustic poet's keen appreciation of the singular
virility of the great Sicilian idyllist, and his warm
recognition of Spenser then almost forgotten by
English pastoralists, are fully set forth in his preface
to the *Shepherd's Week*.

Gay has managed to fill up the Virgillian outline

with all the homeliest details of English country
life, thus showing their incongruity with the Latin
form of the conventional pastoral. There is a
marvellous degree of familiarity with every side of
rural life, and many a picture is drawn with vigorous
strokes. Like William Browe, Gay was full of
sweet memories from rustic childhood, and though
he has neither the delicacy nor the aerial simplicity
of Browne, he excells him in his concision, pro-
priety, and bright realism of style.

In numerous ways Gay shows himself a student
of nature after the manner of a true poet. He
loved a morning walk in the fields,* and at sunset
he often strolled out on the cliffs at Barnstaple to
watch the glowing colors of the evening sky, and
the late beauty of the unclouded twilight, while the
silver moon marked a glittering path along the sea.†
He was one of the first pastoralists to put on record
his delight in a walk to enjoy the beauty of nature,
and he gives us one of the earliest appreciative
mentions of the ocean.

Moreover, Gay was one of the few poets able to
see in mountains an attractive feature of the landscape, and he notes with feeling their lengthened
shadows across the meadows on a late afternoon.
He fixes his interested gaze on the long flight of
crows seeking the woods at sunset; he observes
how the streams are wrinkled by the fresh breeze,
the yellow showers of autumn leaves, and thinks
much of moonlight and starry skies. Gay also
knows the birds, the flowers and the trees with a
sweet definiteness that gives him an important place
among pastoral poets who showed a genuine feeling
for nature.

---

* Edmund Gosse " Gossip in a Library ", p 123.
† Gay, " Rural Sports " 1 : 99.

Notwithstanding all that has been said against the attitude of eighteenth century poetry toward nature, there is on the whole a considerable intensity of feeling for rural scenes, and a fairly elevated range of observation and description, though it is in poetry other than pastoral, that this deeper nature-feeling is to be found. In the verse of Thomson, Burns, Collins, Cowper, and in *The Shepherd's Week* of Allan Ramsay,—a dramatic pastoral,—we note an evident and definite breaking with classicism, and the dawn of the Naturalistic School which soon absorbed the more delicate fancies of pastoral idealization. Those who in the past were accustomed to find escape from the tedious in-door life of a highly artificial society by breathing the etherialized atmosphere of arcadian nymphs and weeping deities, now turned for fresh air to the farms and fields of a raw naturalism, or gratified their love of idealization in the mysteries of Romanticism. At the rise of democracy the worship of the eternal feminine ceased, and with the disintegration of classes and the decay of chivalry, the soul of the pastoral passed away.

CHAPTER XI

THE FEELING FOR NATURE
AND THE DECLINE OF THE PASTORAL

THERE came a time when the graceful muse of Pastoral Poetry began to decline ; and no poet of adequate genius arose to rescue her from the fatal affection that was her undoing. The vanishing of this fair virgin who for more than two thousand years had been the most innocent and alluring delight of literature, has about it sufficient pathos to lend interest to the reason why.

The purpose of her life had been noble and she had an honorable history. She had lived to idealize and therefore to elevate and beautify the common things of life. Our brief survey of her history in relation to nature, does something to reveal the attitude of the world's more cultivated minds to the meaning of life. So long as this attitude continued to be one born of poetry, the pastoral remained sane and healthful as a mode of literature. But with the increasing sophistry of civilization and the plutocracy of cities, the attitude of poetry to nature became extremely sensuous, selfish, and more or less unæsthetic. Consequently a species of poetry whose virgin simplicity and charm involved the very loftiest quality of poetic insight and pure altruism, quickly lost favor with an age incapable of entering into its ravishing æsthetic delight in idealized womanhood and her human environment.

The trend of the æsthetic mind toward the idealization of nature and man, is most agreeable to the genius of poetry, and was doubtless fostered by that mythology* which owed its charm to the poetic habit of personifying and idealizing natural objects. Among the Greeks mythology readily offered to the imagination of poets an opening to the mystery of the unknown, and became a convenient means of poetically viewing nature.

The Greek pastoral was therefore a natural development of the idyl which was a little picture of some natural scene or incident. The poet in due sympathy with the happy lovers, saw something more in his little picture, than is revealed to a merely sensuous vision; and under the influence of this idealizing tendency, his idyl became a pastoral. The idyl was to Greek literature what the pictures on pottery were to Greek plastic art: a studied and well designed picture intended to leave upon the mind a like æsthetic effect to the bass-reliefs and vases of Greek art. Action is represented at a decisive moment in its evolution, as by the snapshot of a camera,—and the beautiful forms are so grouped that the mind easily interprets the meaning. Now what these exquisite miniatures did for Greek art, the pastoralists tried to do for literature.

Nature in her more poetic forms and moods became the background for human action and emotion, and speaks only as she can illustrate one or both of these. Nature is not regarded as something apart from man or worthy of love in herself; man is looked upon as on the earth if not of it. And thus the descriptions of Theocritus express with magical felicity the form and movement of the outward world, but only to show the beauty of love in its human relation: the exquisite blooming of manhood and womanhood; and so his pastorals are a mass of natural blossoms still fresh and sweet and beautiful,—

---

* H. W. Mabie, "Essays in Nature and Culture" p. 84.

" Violets, daffodils, and the lily bell
That trembling laughter fills".

Hence the pastoral, more perhaps, than any other
kind of poetry reflected the fashions, features and
fancies of the periods in which it flourished. It
informs us how in other times than those of high
æsthetic effort and artistic appreciation, it lost
the simplicity and naïve charm of the Sicilian
meadows, and revelled in the wild and extravagant
tastes that characterized the society of such times
as those of Louis the XIVth or of even the English
Elizabeth. Yet in the midst of its impulsive and
passionate childishness, with a gay fondness for
games, music and story, the pastoral never departed
fully from the sweet quality of finding happiness
only in the May-time when youths and maidens
can no more help running and dancing over the
grass, than sunbeams can refrain from flashing
over a brook.

The idealization of nature and the love of song
have always been closely associated; and some
of the most delightful of pastoral lyrics have been
set to music. The alliance of the pastoral with
music was only natural, since both suggest the
same sweet harmonies and nameless longings to
the mind, leaving the conscience and the will
undisturbed. But the passion for sensuous nature
in music has always been attended by the same
result as the like passion in poetry : the exhaltation
of the material at the expense of the spiritual.
Such a course, whether in literature or life, inevit-
ably leads to petrifaction on the one hand or inanity
on the other. Witness the pseudo-classicism of the
reign of Anne, or the drivelling imbecility of verse
in the time of Suckling.

It is only as the external world is subordinated to the appeal of the inner man that true art breathes freely.[1] It was but natural, therefore, that as devotion to the material side of things increased and poetry appealed more and more to the senses, that a mode which depended upon the love of delicate idealization should decline.

If the sensuousness of the later English pastoralists had been occupied with anything above the merely puerile and inane, the fair bucolic muse might have survived the cold shroud of classicism that enfolded her. The poets of the time exhibit none of that exultation in sea and storm so characteristic of the earlier poets of England. Spring and the pleasant uplands become the season and sphere of pastoral effusion, because with these was associated the life of gaiety and ease. But beyond this aspect of nature the poets do not dare to venture; and perhaps with wise precaution. For it requires a rare imagination and a consummate genius to depict poetically the grandest and sublimest of natural scenes. All that even the greatest can say is, " how beautiful ; how wonderful ", and then relapse into becoming silence. It is evident that the ethical sensitiveness and refinement necessary to a full and exquisite expression of the sublime and beautiful in nature, had been either lost, or was not yet developed to the necessary degree of poetic emotion.

Doubtless the English pastoralist was too much under the influence of the Italian poets who always humanised nature before they could see in it anything worthy of interest. Even the painters find no natural scene perfectly natural without a Salon or the

---

1. Victor de Laprade, " La Sentiment de la Nature ", 1868.

Court of a palace.* Indeed Italian poetry and painting have never shown that enjoyment in natural beauty out of doors, to which the Teutonic people have always been so susceptible. The dominant standards of the time were utilitarian, and the ideal of beauty that prevailed involved the ascendancy of order, symmetry, and arrangement. The prejudice against mountains was that they were useless, and therefore a deformity on the face of the earth. Their pronounced irregularity of outline, and the vast shapeless mass of the sea, were features alike unacceptable to the artistic consciousness of the time. The suggestion of mystery and remote irresistibility of power, that accompanied the contemplation of the vast or the unknown, was still more distasteful to the poets of the later pastoral. " From the writers of this time," says an eminent German critic, " no description has reached us of the eternal Alpine snows that redden every eve and early morn ; nor of the beauty of the blue glaciers, and the magnificence of the Swiss landscape. The poets and statesmen who were continually travelling through Helvetia on their way to Gaul 'see none of nature's romantic beauty by the way,

---

* L' homme ne s'interessait pas aux objects inanimès ,il ne leur reconnaissait pas une âme et une beautè propre ; ne servaient que de fond au tableau, fond vague et d'importance moins qu' accessoire. Toute l'attention etait occupèe par le tableau lui même, c'est-a dire par l'intrigue et le drame humain. Pour reporter quelque partie de cette attention sur les arbres, les eaux, le paysage, il fallait les humaniser, leur ôter, leur form et leur disposition naturelle, leur air 'sauvagè, l'apparance du disordre et du dèsert, leur donner autant que possible l'aspect d'im salon, et un galerie à colonnades, d'une grande lour de palais "— : Taine, " Voyage en Italie," Tome I : p231

mentioning only the difficulties of the impassible roads."*

And Biese in commenting on Petrarch's letter describing his ascent of a high mountain which tempted him into a worldly admiration of its vastness and sublimity, looks upon the poet's remarks as the first faint gleam of a pure modern enjoyment of nature, though mixed with what Biese terms a " dogmaticascetic " introspection which affords an insight into the divided heart of a man as he stands at the parting of the ways of the mediæval and the modern world.† The spirit of the past seemed to stand in revolt against the birth of the modern feeling for nature.

It would be a mistake, however, to conclude that there was no deeper feeling for nature than is revealed in pastoral poetry. As one goes through the writings of the poets, one finds here and there unmistakable evidence of many a latent sympathy that never found adequate expression. The desire for full expression was discouraged by the lack of convenient means for publication, and this in the

---

* " Von dem ewigen Schnee der Alpen, wenn sie sich am Abend oder am frühen Morgen röthen, von der Schönheit des blauen Gletscher-Eises, von der grossartigen Natur der schweizerischen Landschaft ist keine Schilderung aus dem Alterthum auf uns gekommen; und doch gingen ununterbrochen Staatsmänner, ...und in ihrem Gefolge Litteraten durch Helvetien nach Gallien. Alle diese Reisenden wissen nur über die unfahrbaren scheusslichen Wege zu klagen ; das Romantische der Naturscenen beschäftigte ;—Humboldt, Kosmos 2 : 16.

† " Und somit eröffnet uns dieser Brief, mit seiner Mischung reinen, modernen Naturgennses und dogmatichasketischer Rüchhelinnung, einen Blick in ein zwiespättikes Herz eines an der Wende zweier Zeiten stehenden Menschen ; es reagiert gleichsam der mittelalterriche Geist wider die aufkeimende moderne Empfindung ",—Biese,— " Die Entwickelung des Naturgefühls. p. 151.

case of true poets, notwithstanding the dictum of Mr. John Stuart Mill, that he who thinks of his audience is no poet. It is difficult to do what no one is doing ; the pastoralists lacked contemporary inspiration and example in the domain of nature :—

> " We're made so that we love
> First when we see them painted, things we have passed
> Perhaps a hundred times, nor cared to see ...."*

Thus a people like the English in whose wild free heart still beat some echoes of the Vikings who loved not only love and chivalry with their youths and maidens, but also the mysterious terror of oceans and floods, the subduing charm of the woods, the majesty of the hills that hold in their dim recesses the secrets of light and atmosphere, the infinite variety of landscape never imitative or repetitious but always appealing to the imagination with some fresh and unsuspected loveliness,—such a people naturally failed to maintain appreciation of a mode of poetry which had come to have respect unto none of these things. When the pastoral lost the nameless charm of high poetic thought and became a mere mirage of rusticity, exulting in fancies marked by neither beauty, faith, nor passion, devoid of anything that pertained to a living possibility,— it died a natural death.

But the poetry of the pastoral, and the love of idealized nature for which it stood, did not die. The fear of being countrified, which settled down like a nightmare on the poetry of the eighteenth century, was passing away, and the feelings of the bucolic muse found fresh channels in such writings as the village tales of Crabbe, and the immortal lyrics of

---

* Browning : " Fra Lippo Lippi ".

the Scottish ploughman, Burns. Wordsworth reasserted the claims of natural simplicity and love of country scenes, and Tennyson and Barnes have found in humble country homes the subject of high poetic contemplation, while the many dialect poems of both England and America reveal a sensuous charm of rustic loveliness that still keeps alive the Theocritean passion of perfect truth to nature.

THE END

BIBLIOGRAPHY

In addition to the authors whose writings have been treated or referred to in the body of this volume, the following works have been found suggestive :

Bancroft, G. *History of Spanish Literature.*
Brunhuber, K. Sir Phillip Sidney's *Arcadia und ihre Nachläufer*, Nürnberg, 1903.
Beers, A. H. *The English Romantic Movement.*
Bosanquet. *History of Aestheic.*
Biese, A. *Die Entwickelung des Naturgefühls bei den Griechen.* Kiel, 1882. *Bei den Römern*, Keil, 1884. *Im Mittelalter und in der Newzeit.* Leipzig, 1888. *Die poëtische Naturbeseelung bei den Greichen.* 1890.

Chambers. E. K. *English Pastorals*, with an Introduction, 1795.
Courthope, W. J. *History of English Poetry ;* five volumes.

Dennis. *The Age of Pope.*
Dowden, E. *Poetical Feeling for Nature.* Contemp. Rev. 2 : 535. *Studies in Literature.* London, 1889
Dilthey, W. *Geschicte d. Philos* Vol II. 1889.
Drees, H. *Die poetische Naturbetrachtung in den Liedern der deutchen Minnesänger.* 1888.

Fillimore, C. *History of Italian Literature.*
Friedlander, L. *Das interesse für Natur und das Naturgefuhl überhaupt. Die Entwickelung d Gefühls für d Romantische in d. Natur im Gegensatz zum antiken Naturgefühl.* Vol. II, p. 170 1881.
Fitzmaurice-Kelly, J. *History of Spanish Literature.* 1898.

Garnett, R. *History of Italian Literature.* 1898.
Gosse, E. Essay on *English Pastoral Poetry.*
Gerber, A. *Naturpersonification in Poesie.*

Grosse, E. *Uber Naturanschaung d. alten griechischen una romischen Dichter.* 1890.
Greg, W. W. *English Pastoral Poetry and Drama.* London, 1906.

Humboldt. *Kosmos* 2 : 16
Hereford, C. H. *Spenser : Shepherds Calendar,* with introduction and notes. London, 1897.
Hensek. K. *Uber das Naturgefuhl in alter und neuer Poesie.*

Jacobs, J. *Daphnis and Chloe.* London, 1890.
Jebb. *Greek Literature.*
Jusserand J. J. *The English Novel in the Time Of Shakespear.*

Lang, A. *Theocritus, Bion and Moschus ;* with an excellent introduction on Alexandrine poetry. London 1889
Landau, Marcus, *Giovanni Bocaccio, sua vita e sue opere.* 1881.
Laprade, V. *Hist. du Sentiment de la Natur.* Paris, 1883.
Luning, O. *Die Natur, ihre Auffassung und poetische Verwendung et cet.* Zurich. 1889.

Mabie, H. W. *Essays on Nature and Culture.*
Macri Leone, F. *La Bucolica latina nella letteratura italiana del secolo XIV, con una introduzione sulla bucolica latina nel medioevo.* Torino, 1889.
Masteran. *Age of Milton.*
Moorman, F. W. *The Interpretation of Nature in English Poetry from Beowulf to Shakespeare ;* also his monograph on William Browne. Strassburg (Quellen und Forschungen) 1897.
Moggridge, W. Essay on *The Idyllic Poets.* Dublin Review.
Minto, W. *Characteristics of the English Poets.*
McKail, J. W. *The Greek Poets.*

Planck, H. *Die Entwinckelung des Naturgefühls im Alterthum.* Stuttgart, 1891.
Posnett, H. M. *Comparative Literature.*

Phelps. *The English Romantic Movement.*
Perry. *Eighteenth Century Literature.*
Petit de Julleville, L. *Histoire de la Langue et de la Litterature française.* 8 vols. Paris, 1899.

Raleigh, W. *The English Novel.* London, 1895.
Rennert, H. A. *The Spanish Pastoral Romances.* Pub. of Mod. Lang. Association of America. vol. vii, pp. 1—119.
Roberts, C. G. D. *Pastoral Elegies :* a Review article.
Ruberto, L. *Egloghe del Petvarca.* Bologna. 1879.

Schelling, F. E. *Seventeenth Century Lyrics. Elizabethan Lyrics. Elizabethan Drama.* New York, 1908.
Sommer, H. O. *Erster Versuch über die englische Hirtendichtung.* Marburg, 1888.
Straub, W. *Der Natursinn der alten Grieschen.* Stuttgart, 1899.
Symonds, J. A. *Renaissance in Italy. Italian Literature,* vols. iv and v. *Studies of the Greek poets,* London, 1893. *Essays Speculative and Suggestive,* vol. ii.
Saintsbury, Geo. *History of English Literature. History of French Literature.*

Uhland und Morike. *Die Naturlyrik.*
Underhill, J. G. *Spanish Literature in the England of the Tudors.* New York (Columbia University studies)

Veitch, J. *The Feeling for Nature in Scottish Poetry.* Edinburg, 1887.
Voss, E. *Die Natur in der Dichtung des Horaz.,* Düsseldorf, 1889.

Weise, B. and Percopo E. *Geschichte de italienischen Litteratur von den altesten Zeliten bis zur Gegenwart.* Leipzig und Wien, 1889.
Wicksteed, P. H. and Gardner E. G. *Dante's ' Eclogae Latinae '.* Westminster, 1902.
Windscheid K. *Die englische Hirtendichtang von 1579-1625.* Hall, 1895.

ERRATA.

Page 8, Second line from the bottom, insert "*the*" before
  virtue.

  „   9, Sixth line from the bottom, for present read
  Peasant.

  „ 16, Nineth line from the bottom, omit *and.*

  „ 86, for Orcades, road *Arcades.*

  „ 96, in first paragraph, for Browe, read *Browne.*

  „ 97, third line from the bottom, for demoracy, read
  democracy.

  „ 99, Second line of last paragraph, for became read
  becomes.

Trieste

Trieste Publishing has a massive catalogue of classic book titles. Our aim is to provide readers with the highest quality reproductions of fiction and non-fiction literature that has stood the test of time. The many thousands of books in our collection have been sourced from libraries and private collections around the world.

The titles that Trieste Publishing has chosen to be part of the collection have been scanned to simulate the original. Our readers see the books the same way that their first readers did decades or a hundred or more years ago. Books from that period are often spoiled by imperfections that did not exist in the original. Imperfections could be in the form of blurred text, photographs, or missing pages. It is highly unlikely that this would occur with one of our books. Our extensive quality control ensures that the readers of Trieste Publishing's books will be delighted with their purchase. Our staff has thoroughly reviewed every page of all the books in the collection, repairing, or if necessary, rejecting titles that are not of the highest quality. This process ensures that the reader of one of Trieste Publishing's titles receives a volume that faithfully reproduces the original, and to the maximum degree possible, gives them the experience of owning the original work.

We pride ourselves on not only creating a pathway to an extensive reservoir of books of the finest quality, but also providing value to every one of our readers. Generally, Trieste books are purchased singly - on demand, however they may also be purchased in bulk. Readers interested in bulk purchases are invited to contact us directly to enquire about our tailored bulk rates. Email: customerservice@triestepublishing.com

You May Also Like

ISBN: 9780649562527
Paperback: 200 pages
Dimensions: 6.14 x 0.42 x 9.21 inches
Language: eng

Digest of the Law Relating to Tithes and Glebe Lands: Under the Acts of the Sessions of 1891 and 1888

George F. Chambers

ISBN: 9780649606009
Paperback: 176 pages
Dimensions: 5.83 x 0.38 x 8.27 inches
Language: eng

Home and School United in Widening Circles of Inspiration and Service: Home-School-Community-Nation

Mary Van Meter Grice & Elmer Ellsworth Brown & Martin Grove Brumbaught

www.triestepublishing.com

You May Also Like

Mechanical Lubrication

Fred Viall Larkin

ISBN: 9780649070589
Paperback: 135 pages
Dimensions: 6.14 x 0.29 x 9.21 inches
Language: eng

Love's Widowhood and Other Poems

Alfred Austin

ISBN: 9780649640409
Paperback: 168 pages
Dimensions: 6.14 x 0.36 x 9.21 inches
Language: eng

www.triestepublishing.com

You May Also Like

ISBN: 9780649333158
Paperback: 84 pages
Dimensions: 6.14 x 0.17 x 9.21 inches
Language: eng

Report of the Department of Farms and Markets, pp. 5-71

Various

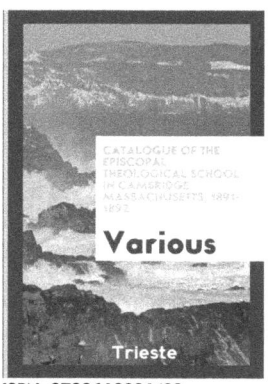

ISBN: 9780649324132
Paperback: 78 pages
Dimensions: 6.14 x 0.16 x 9.21 inches
Language: eng

Catalogue of the Episcopal Theological School in Cambridge Massachusetts, 1891-1892

Various

You May Also Like

ISBN: 9780649352142
Paperback: 88 pages
Dimensions: 6.14 x 0.18 x 9.21 inches
Language: eng

Three Hundred Tested Recipes

Various

ISBN: 9780649419418
Paperback: 108 pages
Dimensions: 6.14 x 0.22 x 9.21 inches
Language: eng

A Basket of Fragments

Anonymous

Find more of our titles on our website. We have a selection of thousands of titles that will interest you. Please visit

www.triestepublishing.com

Lightning Source UK Ltd.
Milton Keynes UK
UKHW01f1148220618
324641UK00006B/732/P